PROJECT ENGINEER: Lyman Coleman, Serendipity House

WRITER FOR NOTES/COMMENTARY: Richard Peace, Gordon Conwell Seminary.

CONTRIBUTORS: Denny Rydberg, University Presbyterian Church, Seattle □ Gordon Fee, Gordon Conwell Seminary, Boston □ Virginia Zachert, Medical College of Georgia, Augusta □ Margaret Coleman, Serendipity House, Denver □ Peter Menconi, Professional Consultants, Denver □ John Mallison, Board of Education, Uniting Church in Australia, Sydney □ John U'Ren, Scripture Union, Melbourne □ Ken Anderson, Synod of South Australia, Uniting Church of Australia, Adelaide □ Anton Baumohl, Scripture Union, Bristol, England □ Lance Pierson, Freelance writer, London □ Emlyn Williams, Scripture Union, Cambridge, England.

PUBLISHER: Serendipity House is a resource community specializing in the equipping of pastors and church leaders for small group ministry in the local church in the English speaking world. A list of training events and resources can be obtained by writing one of the addresses below.

SERENDIPITY U.S.A.
Serendipity House
Box 1012
Littleton, Colorado 80160

Telephone: 800-525-9563

SERENDIPITY AUSTRALIA
Serendipity Christian Resources
P.O. Box 130
West Ryde, NSW 2114

Telephone: SYDNEY 858-1778

SERENDIPITY GREAT BRITAIN
c/o Serendipity U.K.
48 Peterborough Road
London SW6 3EB

Telephone: LONDON 01-731-6544

94 95 96/VIP/10 9 8 7 6 5 4 3 2

Copyright: © 1986, Serendipity Foundation. All rights reserved. Printed in U.S.A.

PHILIPPIANS

A PASTOR DIRECTED STUDY COURSE FOR SMALL GROUPS COMBINING: ■EXPOSITORY TEACHING ■SMALL GROUP SHARING ■PERSONAL APPLICATION

BY LYMAN COLEMAN AND RICHARD PEACE

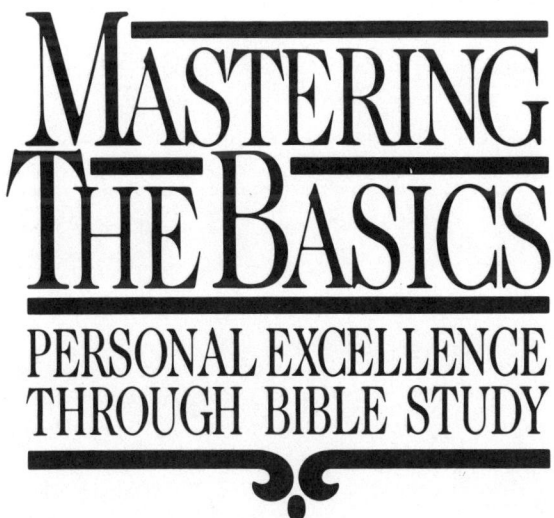

THREE PARTS TO THE PROGRAM: CHOOSE ONE, TWO, OR ALL THREE

This program is designed like an overseas study program with three plans to choose from.

1. Self Study

If you have people in your church who like to travel on their own, at their own speed, and do their own thing as they go, the Self Study Plan is for them. The Study Guide provides home assignments for every unit of study, with a glossary of important words, places and events and a running commentary to help them in their study.

The home assignment worksheet is designed to lead a person step by step through the study, with questions to answer and jot down on the worksheet, and an application to deal with the Scripture passage in his/her own life situation.

If the pastor or teacher is lecturing on this passage on Sunday, this person may wish to attend the lecture and find out what the pastor/teacher has to say about the passage *after* completing the self study.

And if this person wants to get in on a small group after the program has started, this is still a possibility.

In fact, many people who think they prefer traveling on their own end up joining a small group because of the excitement that is generated. The Tower of London is still the Tower of London, but when you go through the Tower of London alone, somehow it is not the same.

2. Group Study

If you have people in your church that love to travel as a group, do things together, see things together and have fun along the way, the Group Study Plan is for them.

In addition to the Self Study home assignments (which you complete on your own), the group meets once a week to share study assignments and enjoy life together.

The group can meet anytime, anywhere during the week, or even before the teaching session on Sunday. The leadership rotates around the group, and leading is not that difficult because a "Group Agenda" with specific sharing questions is provided on the study worksheet for the leader to follow. All the leader has to do is keep to the time recommendations so that the group gets around to sharing the application of the study by the end of the hour.

In the first session of each program the group is asked in the application to decide on goals and group disciplines . . . and to stick to these disciplines.

The group lasts as long as the book they are studying lasts—which can be anywhere from 7 weeks to 28 weeks. If the group wishes to continue after this time, the group will have to choose another book to study and agree on a new set of goals and disciplines.

One of the disciplines we highly recommend is the "empty chair" outreach commitment—to keep an empty chair for newcomers and aggressively go after new members for the group. When the group reaches 8 in number, the group divides into groups of 4 when the time comes for sharing—4 sitting at the kitchen table and 4 at the dining table. When the group reaches 12, the whole group meets together for coffee and then divides into three groups of 4—4 at the dining table, 4 at the kitchen table, and 4 at a card table in the family room, etc.

In other words, one of the exciting possibilities of a group is evangelism, and this is done by inviting new people into the group *every* week.

3. Expository Teaching

To use the analogy of the overseas study program one more time, this plan would be like a super deluxe travel package for the whole church to go along—with the pastor or associate pastor offering special lectures along the way.

In this plan, individuals do their own home assignment, and meet any time during the week with their small groups. Then, on Sunday (or any time that is convenient for all groups) the groups get together to hear the pastor/teacher expound on the material they have already studied. (If you have the teaching session before the groups meet, you take away the fun of sharing their own insights.)

The "Countdown" of pages 8-9 is specifically designed for a church-wide plan. And this book for the Pastor/Teacher is specifically designed to assist the expository teaching preparation. For each teaching unit, there are specific suggestions for teaching the Scripture passage that the small groups have already studied. (If you hold the teaching session before the small groups meet, you take away the excitement of their own self-discovery and sharing).

The Pastor/Teacher has two options for scheduling the teaching. (See the schedule inside of the front cover.) The short schedule can be taught in fewer weeks, but it requires combining some units. The longer schedule allows for one week per unit. (If you want to follow the longer schedule, you may want to switch to a shorter book. Check the back cover for the number of teaching units in each course.)

If you decide on a teaching schedule that requires combining units, the Pastor/Teacher should explain this ahead of time so that the small groups can stay ahead of the teaching in their group sharing.

OVERVIEW

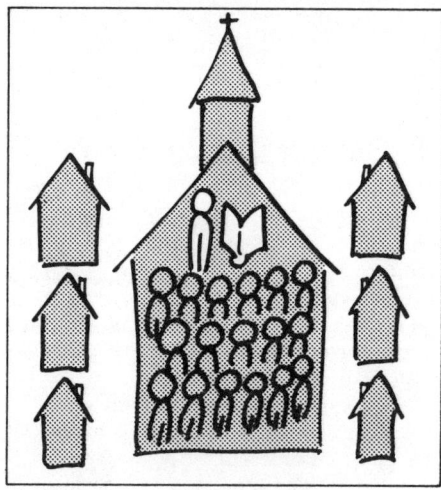

1. On Your Own

The heart of the program is the individual study of Scripture *before* the group session and the teaching session. A person can be in the program without being in a group, by doing the home assignments and attending the teaching sessions.

The home assignment is designed for beginner Bible students. The worksheet for each study unit is in three parts: (a) Read—to get the "bird's eye view" of the passage and jot down on the worksheet your first impressions, (b) Search—to get the "worm's eye view" of the passage, studying the passage verse by verse to find answers for specific questions, and (c) Apply—to find out what God is saying to you in this passage for your life right now.

2. With a Group

The completed home assignment is the basis for the group sharing experience. The "Group Agenda" on the worksheet provides guided questions for the group to share on three levels of sharing: (a) To Begin questions, (b) To Go Deeper questions, and (c) To Close questions.

The leadership rotates around the group, and an "empty chair" is provided for newcomers to the group. When the group reaches eight in number, the group divides into groups of 4 before starting on the sharing—4 around the kitchen table, 4 around the dining table, etc. In this way, the group can keep on growing in number, yet never get too large for good participation in sharing.

3. With a Teacher

All of the small groups come together once a week to hear the pastor or teacher lecture on the same Scripture passage. The teaching session can be at the Sunday school hour, the Sunday morning worship service or one night in the week when the group meetings and teaching session are combined.

People in the church who are not in the program are invited to the teaching session, and can join a small group if they wish to become involved. In fact, some of the test churches in this program found that the best way to start groups in the program was to begin the teaching of a Book of Scripture and invite people to join a group and "study" along."

"We started with seven people in a pilot group last summer. Now we have over two hundred people in twenty two groups with new people joining every day. I have never seen anything like this before.

DR. DICK HAMLIN,
SR. PASTOR
SHEPHERD OF THE VALLEY
LUTHERAN CHURCH,
PHOENIX, AZ

....enthusiasm over the Scripture and subsequent interaction in small groups is outstanding.

DAVE JOHNSON, MINISTER
TO COLLEGE STUDENTS,
GRACE CHAPEL,
LEXINGTON, MA

VITAL FACTS

GOAL: Pastor-directed, integrated, church-wide program for Bible study groups and expository teaching.

COMPONENTS:
- ☐ Expository teaching
- ☐ Personal Bible study
- ☐ Bible study groups

BIBLE KNOWLEDGE REQUIRED: None

TIME COMMITMENTS:
- ☐ For personal study/30 minutes per week
- ☐ For group study/30-45 minutes per week
- ☐ For teaching session/30-45 minutes per week

POTENTIAL CHURCH INVOLVEMENT: Unlimited

EVANGELISM POTENTIAL: Enormous. Everyone has a keen desire in the Bible. The chance to hear good expository teaching, plus the opportunity to belong to a small group is a very attractive package.

COURSES AND DURATION: Each course has two schedule options in weeks.
- ☐ Ephesians: 7 or 13 weeks
- ☐ James: 7 or 13 weeks
- ☐ Romans: 13 or 28 weeks
- ☐ Philippians: 7 or 13 weeks
- ☐ 1 Corinthians 13 or 27 weeks
- ☐ Timothy: 7 or 13 weeks
- ☐ 1 Peter: 7 or 13 weeks
- ☐ 1 John 7 or 13 weeks
- ☐ Revelation: 13 or 28 weeks
- ☐ Mark (Early Ministry): 13 or 28 weeks
- ☐ Mark (Later Ministry): 13 or 28 weeks

Here is a strategy for spiritual growth and numerical growth combined.

CARL GEORGE, DIRECTOR
CHARLES E. FULLER
INSTITUTE OF
EVANGELISM AND
CHURCH GROWTH,
PASADENA, CA

We were able to start fifteen groups with people who had never led a group before because the structure of the program makes leading a group easy.

CARLA BJORK,
COORDINATOR,
COVENANT GROUPS,
MENLO PARK
PRESBYTERIAN CHURCH,
MENLO PARK, CA

People are coming to church prepared to worship because they have already studied the Scripture passage in their group.

PASTOR ED NELSON,
FIRST CHURCH OF GOD
FT. COLLINS, CO

HOW TO GET STARTED

If you decide on the (1) Self Study or the (2) Group Study Plans as described in the previous section, the organization is relatively simple.

You invite everyone in the church to an Orientation Night to learn about the program and get acquainted with the material. If a person wishes to do the program as a Self Study, he/she can purchase the Study Guide and proceed with the study on his/her own.

If a group or several groups of people wish to do the Group Study, each small group decides upon the book in the Bible they want to study and orders the Study Guides for this particular course. (See the courses on back cover.)

If you want to use the third plan—Church-wide Groups With Pastoral Teaching—with all of the groups studying the same book in Scripture, the Pastor/Teacher must select the Book of Scripture to teach and decide how to start the program. Here are two choices: (a) The Amoeba Approach, or (b) The "Big Bang" Approach.

The Amoeba Approach

The easiest way to get the church-wide program started is to have the pastor announce the kick off week when the teaching of a particular book in this program is going to start, and invite everyone who wants to belong to a study group to sign up. The pastor/teacher can meet with these people and explain the program.

This is the way it all started in one church in the testing program. The pastor announced that he would be started a teaching of 1 Corinthians on January 6, and that anyone who was interested in belonging to a group and studying along with his Sunday teaching could get the Study Guides after the service. The first Sunday, one group asked for the material. The next Sunday, another group wanted "in."

In six weeks, eight groups were participating. In three months, there were twelve . . . and groups are still forming.

The key to this approach is the teaching session at a very convenient time when people can come and hear the book being taught by someone who can make the Bible "come alive." This will entice people who would otherwise be reticent about being in a group to want to get in on the action.

Each week the pastor explains: "If you would like to be a part of a small group and get together to share your own study of the passage *before* I teach it, see So and So for the Study Guide and more details about group possibilities." In fact, this announcement should appear in the bulletin almost every Sunday.

The Big Bang Approach

The second approach is much more systematic and requires a lot more work, but the results are probably more rewarding. In the "Big Bang" Approach, the pastor decides on a Book of Scripture from one of the courses, such as 1 Corinthians or James, and a convenient time in the week when the expository teaching will take place, such as: during the Sunday school hour, or even the Sunday morning worship service. The "Countdown" on the next two pages gives a schedule for a six month period leading up to the start of the program in the church:

☐ Recruiting group leaders/hosts

Continued on page 10

COUNTDOWN FOR A CHURCHWIDE PLAN

6. PASTOR/TEACHER CHOOSES BOOK TO BE STUDIED

Goal: To start thinking about the Book of Scriptures to teach and when.

Before anything else can take place, the pastor or the teacher who has been chosen to do the teaching and assist in the training of the group leaders should decide on the book of Scripture to be studied.

Consideration should be given to the length of time you can devote to the program in the church schedule. The shorter books of the Bible can be taught in 13 weeks—one week per unit—such as Ephesians, James, Philippians, 1 John, etc. If the teaching starts in September, a 13-week course could be finished before Advent (December).

If you are interested in groups lasting through the school year (which is what we recommend), you may wish to pick a longer book with 27 or 28 weeks of study, such as 1 Corinthians or Romans.

The Pastor/Teacher Commentary and the Study Guide for this course should be ordered.

5. PASTOR/TEACHER LEADS PILOT GROUP FOR LEADERS

Goal: To recruit potential group leaders and build a team to run the program.

Potential leaders are personally recruited by the pastor for the pilot group, representing every age bracket and strata of the church: college age, young adult, young couples, singles, etc.

The pilot group meets for six to eight weeks. The sessions are divided equally between practice and planning. For the practice session, the group should be run exactly like an actual group in the program, with the group dividing into smaller groups of 4 and sitting at card tables (or small tables) all over the house. One person in each foursome is assigned to lead the group, using the Group Agenda on the worksheet for that session.

During the planning time at each session, the group regathers to discuss the over-all plans for the church-wide program and divide up the chores.

The pilot group becomes the pool from which leaders are chosen to run the program. The pastor/teacher gets a first-hand experience with the Study Guide material for groups and the excitement of being in a group.

4. PASTOR/TEACHER STARTS ANNOUNCING THE PROGRAM

Goal: To get the word out to the whole church in every possible way.

The word about the program will get around quickly through the people in the pilot group (there is nothing so contagious as an "unofficial news leak").

The official publicity campaign should start about six weeks before the program is to begin with eye-catching posters, fliers, and church bulletin announcements, plus the personal encouragement from the pastor each Sunday.

The pastor should emphasize the big dream of the whole church getting involved together. The three plans for involvement should be explained: (1) Self Study—on your own—plus the Expository Teaching with the pastor, (2) Group Study—with a small group during the week—plus the Expository Teaching with the pastor on Sunday, and (3) Church-wide Groups—throughout the week—plus the Expository Teaching with the pastor.

Every announcement should mention the Information/Orientation Night where everyone can get acquainted with the program.

3. PASTOR/TEACHER HOLDS ORIENTATION NIGHT

Goal: To give people a chance to see the program before deciding to join a group.

The whole church is invited to a pot-luck supper in the church fellowship hall with nursery facilities available for the children and the youth providing baby-sitting for the older kids.

The pastor and members of the pilot group explain the program and share what they have experienced in the pilot group. The Study Guide for the Scripture book that the pastor is going to teach is passed out and the pastor leads everyone in a guided tour of the first few pages of the Study Guide, including the model for personal Bible study and group sharing from Unit One (on page 10 in the Study Guide).

The pastor introduces the group leaders who have volunteered to "host" a group and explains the procedure for joining a group in this program.

This Information Night should be scheduled about two weeks before the first Expository Teaching session—to give the small groups a week to "sign-up" and a week to have their own group meeting before the teaching session.

A complete agenda for this Orientation Night is given on pages 12-15.

2. PASTOR/TEACHER LAUNCH GROUP SIGN-UP WEEK

Goal: To register and assign as many people as possible to groups before the Expository Teaching begins.

The week following the Orientation Night is designated as "sign-up week" for the program, inviting everyone to "call a few friends" during the week and finalize plans by the following Sunday (at least one week before the Expository Teaching begins).

(Note: If you used the Group Preference Questionnaire—page 11—you can use this information for assigning people to groups according to their preference for time, age bracket and interest.)

Study Guides are given out as people sign up and money collected for the book. If a person was not at the Information Night, the study assignment for the first session is explained so that the person can do the homework for the first session.

Having a special one-week push will help to emphasize the importance of getting started BEFORE the first Expository Teaching session.

1. SMALL GROUPS AND EXPOSITORY TEACHING BEGIN

Goal: To start all of the groups at the same time in sync with the Expository Teaching.

Kick-off week begins with the small groups meeting throughout the week or all at the same time immediately before the Expository Teaching session with the pastor/teacher.

Groups that did not receive their Study Guides or complete the home assignment before this session use the time to go over the Bible study for Unit One together, answering the questions on the spot.

The group leader divides the group into 4's and appoints one person in each foursome as the leader. This person uses the questions under Group Agenda on the worksheet in the Study Guide to lead the discussion.

The last few minutes of the group meeting is spent working on the group goals and disciplines that are suggested in the Bible study for Unit One under "Apply."

All of the small groups gather for the Expository Teaching session and the pastor/teacher encourages the groups to keep growing.

Continued from page 7

- ☐ Publicizing the program
- ☐ Holding an Orientation Night
- ☐ Matching people with groups
- ☐ Starting the teaching

The advantage of this approach is the church-wide family feeling that the program generates. People who normally do not get involved in groups will join a group because they want to cooperate with the program, and suddenly they will find themselves in a life-changing experience. Conversely, a person who is really not too interested in serious Bible study will find their appetite for Scripture whetted because of their group involvement.

There is also a healthy control that the pastor and board can exercise over the groups in this approach that can head off some of the problems of groups.

Pilot Group

If you are undecided about the program and wish to "test the waters" before committing your church to a particular plan of action, you may want to consider holding a pilot group.

Here, the pastor or associate pastor would recruit some key people to belong to a pilot group for a few weeks, using the Study Guide of one of the courses. Intentionally choose people for the group who represent a wide range of the church life. Meet in a home where you can have several card tables—so that the people can sit in 4's close together—just like the model recommended in the program. Ask everyone to do the home assignment and have one person in each foursome take the

---

CHURCH BULLETIN ANNOUNCEMENT

"MASTERING THE BASICS"

This _____ (season), our church will launch a church-wide program for achieving excellence in Bible study. It combines three disciplines and three dimensions in Bible study: (1) expository teaching, (2) self study and (3) group study.

EXPOSITORY TEACHING. Our pastor (or whoever it is) will be teaching through the book of _____(name of Scripture book) starting on_____(day) mornings (or evenings) at the _____(hour) for_____(weeks). You are welcome to attend these lectures, even if you cannot participate in the rest of the program.

SELF-STUDY. For a deeper experience, you are invited to do your own study of the Scripture before attending the Expository teaching session. A study guide on the book of _____(name of Scripture book to be studied) will help you prepare for the teaching session by providing an inductive Bible study questionnaire to fill out, with a glossary of terms and a running commentary on the study passage.

GROUP STUDY. For a maximum growth experience, you can also join a small group and go over your Bible study together before attending the teaching session. The study guide also provides complete instructions for the group meeting, with guided questions to help share your personal study and grow together as a group.

ORIENTATION NIGHT

If you are interested in any aspect of this program, you are invited to attend an orientation night on _____ (day), _____ (date). The pastor and _____ (people involved in planning) will be available to explain the program and introduce you to the materials.

Refreshments (or pot luck supper) will be served, starting at _____ (time) in the _____ (place). Babysitting will be available for those with small children.

Here is an opportunity for our whole church to get involved in something that will bind us together as a family. Please pray with us for this new step in our life together.

MORE INFORMATION

For more information, call the church office or one of the committee to learn more about this exciting opportunity: Church Office _____ (Phone) or _____ (name), _____ (phone) or _____ (name) _____ (phone)

leadership role for their foursome. Here are some suggestions for the pilot group:

- ☐ Singles—a real gold mine and totally untapped
- ☐ New church members—before they get stale
- ☐ Wife of the pastor—who is tired of playing "second fiddle"
- ☐ Young Christians—who are hungry for growth
- ☐ Way-out radicals—who have turned off the traditional church
- ☐ Troubled parents—who are reaching out for help
- ☐ Busy business people—who respect excellence
- ☐ Spiritual widows—who have no fellowship at home
- ☐ Society women—who are tired of bridge
- ☐ Young mothers—who need to get out of the house
- ☐ Sponsors of the Youth Group—who never have anything for their own growth
- ☐ Church drop-outs—who are still looking for God

Before the pilot group is finished, you will not only have decided on the plan you want to use in your church, but you will probably have all the leaders you can use for your initial groups. In fact, if it runs according to our experience, you will have people asking how they can get into a group before you even announce the program.

Nothing travels as fast as a rumor. Everybody wants to get in on something exciting. And down underneath, everybody is searching for a deeper walk with God. It is simply a matter of finding the nerve and pressing it.

GROUP PREFERENCE QUESTIONNAIRE

"MASTERING THE BASICS"

To assist the coordinator for small groups in planning for the church-wide program for Bible study through the book of _____ (Scripture book to be studied), beginning the week of _____ (date), please take a few minutes and complete the questionnaire below and return to the church office.

The small groups will share their study of the Scripture passage before the pastor (or whoever is teaching) teaches the passage on _____.

GROUP PREFERENCE: What kind of group would you prefer to belong to?
☐ Men's ☐ Women's ☐ Couples ☐ Mixed ☐ Singles ☐ Business/Professional

AGE PREFERENCE: What age bracket would you like to be a part of in a group?
☐ Senior high ☐ College ☐ 20-30 ☐ 30-40 ☐ 40-50 ☐ 50 and over Mixed ages

INTEREST FACTOR: What other factors would you like to consider? (Check any)
☐ Newly married ☐ Young children ☐ Teenage children ☐ Single Parent
☐ Widowed ☐ Mid-life career change ☐ Working mother/return to college

GROUP MEETINGS: What would be the best time for you to meet?
☐ Early morning ☐ During the day ☐ At night ☐ Saturday ☐ Sunday school hour
☐ Sunday night ☐ _____

HOST: Would you be willing to host a group in your home? ☐ Yes ☐ No

All groups will begin on the week of _____ date, with the Expository Teaching on the passage by the pastor (or whoever is doing the teaching) beginning on _____ (day) _____ (date) at _____ (time) in the _____ (place). The small groups should try to start before the first teaching session, so that the groups can share their study of the passage before the teaching session.

If you have any questions, please contact the church office at _____ (phone) or one of the coordinators: _____ (name) _____ (phone), etc.

Name: _____

Address: _____ Phone: _____

ORIENTATION NIGHT FOR EVERYONE

OBJECTIVES:

- To explain the program and give a brief introduction to the book that will be studied.
- To give out the Study Guide for the program and lead everyone in a guided tour of the first few pages.
- To introduce the hosts/group leaders and explain the various options for group meetings.
- To invite people to sign up for a group and meet with their leader/host.
- To introduce the Book of Scripture that is going to be studied.
- To emphasize the "empty chair" approach to group growth.

SETTING: Fellowship hall with space for a pot-luck supper and movable chairs that can be rearranged in groups if there is time for a brief get-acquainted time (optional).

NAME TAGS: Stick-on name tags and magic markers at the door for people to use for this evening.

TIME: 60 minutes, plus time for the pot-luck supper.

LEADERS: Pastor, coordinators, and group leaders/hosts.

MATERIALS REQUIRED:

- Covered dish, pot-luck supper
- Stick-on name tags
- Study Guides for everyone. (Do not have the people write in the books unless they are going to buy one).

- ☐ Pencils
- ☐ Overhead projector to explain the program.

AGENDA:

- ☐ Welcome from Pastor/5 Minutes
- ☐ Guided Tour of Study Guide/10 Minutes
- ☐ Introduction to Book of Scripture To Be Studied/15 Minutes
- ☐ Introduction of Groups Leaders/Hosts/5 Minutes
- ☐ Group Meetings/15 Minutes (Optional)
- ☐ Wrap up and Questions/10 Minutes

Welcome from Pastor/ 5 Minutes

Welcome the group and introduce them to the dream of a church-wide program to get to know the Word of God and one another in a deeper way. Explain briefly the three-dimensional approach to the study of Scripture in this program: (1) self study, (2) group study, and (3) expository teaching.

If the pastor is going to be doing the Expository Teaching, announce the book you will be teaching; how many weeks you will be teaching the book, and invite everyone to study along with you in this exciting adventure.

Guided Tour of Study Guide/ 10 Minutes

Pass out the Study Guide (participants' book) to everyone. Say something like, "This is the Study Guide for the Book of _____ (Scripture book) which I will be teaching. This Study Guide will help you get the most out of this program, whether you are doing the study on your own or with a group.

Inside Front Cover. Look inside the front cover in your book at the schedule." (Explain which schedule you are going to use.) "We will start the Expository Teaching on ____(date) and continue for ___ weeks through _____ (date)."

Page 5: "Now, turn over to page 5 in your Study Guide and take a look at the three options you have for participating in this program." (Take a moment and explain in your own way the three plans: Self Study, Group Study and Church-wide groups with the Expository Teachings on Sunday. Go over all of the questions on page 7 and ask if there are any more questions.)

Page 10: "Now, let's take a moment and look at the Bible study approach which you will find on page 10 (or 12) for Unit One. Notice that there are three phases to the Bible study: (1) Read—

twice—and jot down your first impressions of the passage. This is to give you a 'bird's eye view' of the passage; (2) Search—verse by verse—looking for answers to the questions and jotting down your results. This would be a 'worm's eye view' of the passage; and (3) Apply—making the passage personal to your own life at the moment.

"The Scripture passage is printed right next to the worksheet, and if you do not have your own Bible dictionary, turn the page and look at the Notes. You will find here the key words, people and places explained, plus a running commentary on the passage.

"Before we move on, turn back to the Bible study a moment and notice the far right column—Group Agenda. Here is the agenda for the group leader to use when you get together to share the Bible study. Note how the agenda has sharing questions on three levels: (1) To begin, (2) To go deeper, and (3) To close. With these questions, anyone can lead the group. In fact, the program recommends that the leadership of the group rotate each week—a different person taking responsibility in turn."

Introduction of Group Leaders/ 5 Minutes

Pause here to introduce the coordinators of the program and the group leaders. Explain how you went about choosing the leaders in the hope of reaching out to every segment of the church: college, youth adult, singles, couples, business/professional people, housewives, mid-wives, and everybody else that needs to be part of this program.

Explain their function by saying something like: "The word leader is probably not the right word to use. A better word might be group convener or host. The leadership of the group actually rotates around the group, each person taking a turn. (With the questions provided in the Group Agenda on the worksheet, it is simply a matter of choosing questions and keeping the group from talking too long.)

"The group meetings can take place any time, any where, as long as the meeting occurs *before* the teaching session.

"And the group can consist of any configurations: ☐ All men ☐ All women ☐ College age ☐ Singles ☐ Newly married ☐ Middle aged ☐ Mixed ages ☐ Business/professional people ☐ Couples with small children (with baby-sitting) ☐ Single parents ☐ Parents of teenagers, etc.

"The important thing is to find a group which is convenient in your time schedule: ☐ Breakfast on your way to work ☐ During the day for lunch ☐ In the evening for coffee ☐ Close to your neighborhood ☐ At the Sunday school hour ☐ On Sunday evening after church ☐ In place of the mid-week service, etc.

Hopefully, you will have a pretty good idea from talking with prospects before this evening what some good suggestions would be for meeting times and you can simply announce the times and the group leaders for these times.

Or you may want to ask the people to cluster for a few minutes right now and discuss what would be the best time for the group to meet: the college age with the college age group leader, the men who want to meet as a men's group, the women who want to meet during the day, etc.

Four people is a crowd for good discussion. Be sure to split into 4's and ask one person in each foursome to be the leader. This model is crucial.

Group Meetings (Optional)/ 15 Minutes

This part of the agenda is optional because you may not want to take time right now for these meetings. If not, you may want to use the time outlining on the blackboard or map of the area some of the possibilities for groups and let the people think about it . . . or indicate their preference by turning in the questionnaire on page 11 . . . and allow the coordinators to do the assigning to groups with the group leaders after the session.

Introduction to the Book for Study/ 15 Minutes

Call everyone back together for a brief introduction to the book you are going to study in this program. You can refer to some of the material in the Introduction in the Study Guide, plus any visuals that you find helpful.

Call attention again to the home assignment in the Study Guide for Unit One and explain that you will be teaching this passage yourself after their study and group sharing of the passage. (If you intend to cover more than one unit in your first lecture, you need to ask the people to cover the same units in their preparation.)

Wrap Up and Questions/ 10 Minutes

Ask everyone to turn back one more time to the APPLY section in the Bible study for Unit One on page 11 (or 13) in the Study Guide. Read over the list of disciplines in the last question:

☐ To complete the Bible study home assignment before the group meeting

☐ To attend the group meetings except in cases of emergency

☐ To share in leading the group—taking my turn in rotation

☐ To keep anything that is shared in the group in confidence

☐ To reach out to others who are not in a group and invite them in

☐ To attend the teaching session with the Pastor/Teacher

Remind the group again of the "empty chair" discipline—to always keep an empty chair for newcomers and to divide the group into 4's when the time comes for sharing so that the group never feels too large to have one more.

Remind the group again of the home assignment . . . and if you are covering more than one unit in the first teaching session, remind them of this.

NOTE: If anyone would like to be in a group but was unable to find a group to fit his/her time schedule, invite this person to give you his/her name and see to it that this person is contacted.

QUESTIONS

1. *What is so different about this Bible study program?* The integrated approach to Scripture: (1) on your own, (2) with your small group, and (3) with your pastor/teacher.

2. *Do you do all three at once?* No. You do your personal study at home before the small group meeting. The small group meetings and the teaching session with the pastor/teacher can be on the same night, or the small group can meet during the week and have the teaching session at another time when all groups meet together.

3. *How long does the program last?* It varies depending upon the book of the Bible you are studying and the schedule you are using for this book; i.e., one unit per week, or combining units to shorten the time. See the two options inside the front cover.

4. *Can a person join a group after the program has started?* Yes. In fact, this is the whole purpose of the "empty chair." Each group is committed to inviting newcomers each week to the group.

5. *What do you do when the group gets too large?* You always split into groups of 4 before you start the sharing, such as a group of 4 in the kitchen, a group of 4 in the dining room, and a group of 4 in the living room, etc.

6. *Why does the pastor have to be involved in the program?* People look to the pastor for direction. Unless the pastor is quarterback—or at least the coach on the sidelines—the program will not work.

UNIT 1—Salutation/Philippians 1:1-2

Ready

With a lot of books one reads these days, there is a lot *less* than meets the eye. But with Philippians, the reverse is true. At first glance it seems to be little more than an informal and somewhat meandering conversation between old friends—"Thanks for the gift. Aren't you glad Epaphroditus got better? Oh, by the way, our mutual friend Timothy will be coming to see you. And did you know what has happened since I've been in prison? A lot of really unexpected people have become Christians—palace guards no less. And people from Caesar's own staff. Would you believe it! And this with all those folks who are out there trying to make reputations for themselves as preachers at my expense while I'm stuck here in prison. But it's okay. Our gospel is so big and so powerful, it doesn't matter who tells it. If the word gets out, good results will follow. And what a Person we follow. Can you believe it! He had it all—the jewels of heaven—and he gave it up for us. Would that we could all be that humble and serving. Speaking of which, you two ladies have got to stop the fight. We need you both. The church needs you. The gospel needs you. I need you. But let me tell you who nobody needs—those jerks who are trying to get you all bound up again in rules and regulations. 'Do this. Do that.' Or 'God's not gonna like you.' Don't you believe it. Keep up all the good things you got going for you. That's quite a prize out there. So I gotta go now. I'll come see ya, once I get out of this joint. And, thanks again for the gift. I needed that. And, by the way, rejoice. You hear that? Rejoice. There is a lotta joy out there. You just gotta see it. Cia."

Philippians—a simple book, merely a conversation between old friends, a chat of little substance? As our pseudo-Paul would say, "Don't you believe it." Philippians may look like a simple chat, but it's a chat filled with dynamite. There is great stuff here, but we need to have eyes to see it. We need to look beyond the casualness and seeming "off the cuff" quality. We've got to see into Paul's heart, into what he really wants for these beloved friends, into his vision of what the gospel is all about, into his life circumstances when he wrote. There are great themes here, which is why Philippians is a favorite of so many Christians: life and death, victory over suffering, joy in the face of trauma, humility as the model for life. We need to look carefully lest we miss all this.

This is where you as teacher come in, of course. Your job is to unlock all this for your class. You will have help. There are the notes in the Study Guide, the small group sessions, and all the materials in this book which have been prepared especially for you. But still, in the end, only you can take all this and mold it to the specific needs of your particular class. Only you can sense what it will take for learning to happen. You are going to enjoy teaching Philippians. And, hey—rejoice, okay?

Aim

☐ To describe how the class will be run . . . and then provide the materials and create the structures.

☐ To discuss the anatomy of joy . . . and so begin to understand the central theme of this epistle.

☐ To touch on the background of the book . . . and so begin to grasp the overall structure and aim of the book.

☐ To begin the large group discussion . . . and so help people notice their assumptions about joy as well as their personal agenda for the class.

Fire

Teaching Strategy

The way in which you will teach this first session depends upon what preparation the class has had. If they received their books (and had the week to work through the material in the introduction) and if they spent some time in a small group prior to meeting with you, then you can get on with this session without any further ado. But if, as is likely, this is the first time everyone is meeting together, there will be certain organizational details that need attention. You will have to distribute the Study Guides and you will need to form the small groups. Do not leave these organizational details until the end of the class when you might not have enough time to take care of everything adequately. It is important that class members know exactly how the sessions will be run, what will be expected of them, and how the class will proceed. This reduces anxiety, especially if this sort of adult class is new to them.

But on the other hand, whatever you do, do not take the whole class session to work on organization. *Be sure to spend some time in Philippians.* You want your class to begin to get excited about this amazing epistle. You want to whet their appetites for more. You want them to look forward to session number 2—and you won't get this kind of response if all you do is deal with class structure.

Organizational Details

Begin then, by attending to the following details if this has not already been taken care of:

☐ **Materials:** Distribute a copy of the Study Guide to everyone. Have them leaf through it while you explain its various sections and how it is to be used by them.

17

- **Small Groups:** Form the class into a series of small groups. Discuss how these will function and when they will meet.
- **Teaching Sessions:** Explain how you will conduct the concluding teaching session with the combined groups. Let them know that this will consist of a combination of mini-lectures and large-group discussion.
- **Questions:** Let people ask questions, but do not take too long at this since the teaching/learning process will become clear as they experience it.

Introduction

Typically you will begin each session with a mini-lecture in which you lay out before the class the material which you will cover that day, how this impacts on them, and/or some interesting facet of the passage that will capture their attention. These mini-lectures will be written out for you in this Pastor/Teacher Commentary and enclosed in quotation marks. You can simply read this material aloud to the class or you can use it as the basis for your own introduction. In fact, every time you come across material in quotation marks, this is a sign that it is meant to be presented by you to the class. Notes addressed to you as the teacher (such as these) will not be in quotes.

Once you have attended to all the organizational details, turn the attention of the class to the epistle to the Philippians. If the class has yet to read over the introductory material, and if they have not yet discussed the book in a small group, begin by pointing out that Philippians has been called "the Epistle of Joy" because of the frequency with which Paul sounds this note in these four short chapters. Use as the basis for your remarks the information in the first section of the Introduction in the Study Guide. Then move into the following mini-lecture. (If the class has discussed the book, you can start at this point.)

Begin by saying: "Philippians is a book which we as twentieth-century American church-goers both like and mistrust. We like it because its note of joy reverberates with us. We want joy. We never get enough joy. Anything that can tell us how to find joy we listen to.

"But we also *mistrust* Philippians (though most of us would never admit this publicly). We mistrust it because Paul doesn't tell us how to get rid of pain and problems. As a result, we can't imagine how he can teach us anything about joy because in our minds, joy is what comes when our problems go away.

"I think that for a lot of us, this is what joy is: the absence of the negative. When things are going our way, then we have joy. When they are not, well, joy isn't possible—or so we imagine. But in fact, this is not how joy is understood in the New Testament. Joy is a much stronger word than 'the lack of problems.' It connotes the *presence* of something important, not just the absence of what we don't like. Otherwise Paul could never write as he does here.

"Think about Paul's situation for a moment. He is in prison. To be incarcerated is never pleasant. But for a man as active and as driven as Paul, it must have been doubly hard. There was so much he wanted to do. There were so many people who had not heard the gospel. And yet all he could do was wait, being confined to one small space. And then there was the anxiety. While he had high hopes of being released, this was by no means a certainty. He could just as well remain in jail for years or be sentenced to death. He is obviously thinking about death as it becomes clear in the first chapter. And there was the physical problem. Paul does not say much about this. But reading between the lines here and in others of his letters, it seems likely that he was not a well man. He has this "thorn in the flesh." Whatever this is, chances are it had a physical component. Prison life is never good for one physically, but especially not if you are already unwell when you enter it. There must have been a fair amount of discomfort for Paul. And then there was prison life in general. You are deprived of exercise. The food is probably not too good. Comfort is not characteristic of prison. All in all, being in jail is no fun.

"In the face of his situation, what kind of attitude does Paul display? What would be the tone of a letter *you* wrote from jail? It would probably not be too upbeat. But, as you know, this is not a gloomy letter. Quite the contrary. What Paul expresses in his letter to the Philippians is joy—abundant, uncontainable, overflowing joy.

"Not only is he joyful, but he counsels the Philippians also to be joyful—even though their situation leaves a lot to be desired. This is a church which at that moment had big problems. For one thing, it was not unified. Apparently two key women in the church were at odds with one another and this was causing real problems. Macedonian women were not to be trifled with as will become evident in the course of this study. And if this was not enough, the church was also being forced to deal with false teachers whose errant doctrine was highly destructive. So, this is a church pressed from within and pressed from without and yet Paul says to it: 'Rejoice in the Lord always. I will say it again: Rejoice!'

"How can he say this given his circumstances and theirs? This is what we will want to figure out over the course of this study. We need to know how we can flourish in the midst of adversity. In fact, we need to figure out how Paul can flourish in adversity. You see, in Philippians we have a rare opportunity. We can study a man under stress. And this is no ordinary man, as you know. This is Paul, the apostle of our Lord. This is Paul at the end of his life. This is Paul, the fiery Pharisee who has been transformed into literally a 'new creation.

Joy – Excitement of pleasurable feeling caused by the acquisition or expectation of good.

Grace – Favor, goodwill, or kindness. Disposition to oblige another. The love and favor of God. Divine influence renewing the heart and restraining from sin. A state of reconciliation to God. Mercy, pardon, unmerited favor.

This is Paul who reflects in himself how Christianity expresses itself in the real world. In other words, if we look carefully at Philippians we will discover how it is that Christianity works.

"So in our discussion this session, let's begin with joy, since this is a central theme in the book. Specifically, let's begin with our ideas about joy. All of us have some ideas about joy—what it is, how to get it, how to lose it. And it is important to get in touch with these assumptions. Otherwise, when we hear Paul talking about joy we might read into his remarks what we assume about joy. And this could be widely off the mark. In fact, I suspect that to the degree we have been influenced by our contemporary culture our ideas about joy will differ from how Paul views joy. So to prevent us from filtering everything he says through the grid of our own experience, we need to become aware of what we think about the subject. Then it becomes possible to distinguish between our ideas and Paul's ideas.

"So, let's discuss joy."

Discuss *(5)*

What is Joy?

Ask: When you hear the word "joy," what images spring into your mind? Answers will include examples such as the following:

☐ A little child who just climbed into his grandfather's lap.

☐ An olympic athlete who upon winning a gold medal, throws her head back, raises her arms, and lets out a whoop of joy.

☐ Two lovers walking hand in hand down a beautiful beach in a soft sunset.

☐ A girl you went to high school with whose name was Joy. (This is supposed to be a joke!)

☐ The soap that promises sparkling dishes and smooth hands! (Another joke?)

After you have four or five responses, you might want to analyze these images. Some of them will probably relate to accomplishments, others have to do with positive relationships, still others are fed by the images of joy that we get from television ads. Almost none of these images, I suspect, will be connected with hard times. Obviously, we've got a lot to learn from Paul!

From images, move to memories.

Ask: Now think about your own experience. When have you experienced joy? [You as teacher might want to begin by sharing an experience of joy that you have had.] Ask the class to listen carefully to the various experiences in order to understand what joy is and how it comes.

Ask: Given what we have discussed about joy, what are some of your thoughts about how it is possible to experience joy in the midst of adversity? Answers will include: *Question #4-8*

☐ Joy is often given, not gained.

☐ Joy has its root in commitments that difficulty cannot erase.

☐ Joy often comes unbidden. It simply is there.

☐ In hard times, it is difficult to feel happy but it is possible to know joy.

☐ Joy springs from what is deep within us.

☐ We gain joy when we bring joy.

Background

Your aim in the final section is to give the class a feel for the way in which the book of Philippians is put together. How you do this will depend upon whether or not the group had an opportunity to read the Introduction in the Study Guide.

If the group has not read the Introduction, highlight the key points for them. It is not necessary to go over all the material since they will have an opportunity to read it for themselves during the week. Your aim is to give them a sense of what the book is all about and why it was written.

If the group has read the Introduction, move straight into the following exercise.

Display the following outline on an overhead projector or write it on the chalkboard.

1. Introduction (1:1-11)
II. The Advance of the Gospel: News about Paul and his situation (1:12-26)
III. The Need for Unity: Instructions for the Philippians in their situation (1:27—2:18)
IV. Examples from Three Relationships (2:19—4:9)
V. Conclusion (4:10-23)

Instruct the group to skim the whole epistle to the Philippians in five to ten minutes (depending upon how much time you have available). The Outline will guide them. Remind them that they are asked to skim, not read carefully, the material. Ask them to be alert to what strikes them about this book as they glance through it. When time is up:

Ask: What are your impressions of Philippians? [Obviously, the responses will vary from class to class. Your aim as a teacher is not so much that the class master the structure of the book as it is to get people to begin thinking about it as a whole.] Try to help them see the following points:

☐ This is an informal letter that seems to unfold with little conscious outline. It is more a conversation than a lecture.

(6) Page 6 (of the book)

1 2 3

- Despite his real problems, there are concrete things for which Paul is thankful (their gift, the advance of the gospel, the recovery of Epaphroditus, etc.)
- Both Paul and the Philippians face real problems. Paul is in prison and he has rivals in the church who are jealous of him. The Philippians have not only their internal dissension to worry about but those who would seek to pervert the gospel.
- There is much practical advice in this book about how to live as a Christian.

Remind

Homework
Before you dismiss the class be sure to go over the small group assignments for the next week if you have not already done so. If you are using the 7-week schedule, explain how many units you will be covering during the next session so that they can prepare all the necessary units in the Study Guide.

Reminder/Empty Chair
Remind the class of their covenant to reach out to others who want to be in a Bible study group. Explain how the small groups can stay small for discussion by splitting into groups of four when the time comes for sharing.

Order More Study Guides
If you need more books for newcomers, call Serendipity House TOLL FREE 800-525-9563.

Comment

Joy—The Book
In 1967 William C. Schutz published a book with the title *Joy: Expanding Human Awareness.* It was a best seller. On the cover of the paperback edition it was touted as "The book that made encounter groups famous." Looking at the book today it has the feel of a different era about it. The whole idea of "encounter groups" and "expanding human awareness" sounds a bit strange to our ears. It rings of an age gone by—of hippies and rock music and love-ins; of protest and marches and Vietnam; of a society in upheaval being transformed into something quite different from what we had always assumed to be the "American Way."

However, the central focus of the book—the discovery of joy—is very much alive today. We still want joy. We still suspect that we are missing out on a lot of joy. We still are willing to pay a high price to find joy. I wonder how much Schutz's book—and the movement of which it was a part—created this longing for joy? But that question is too large for us to consider here.

Schutz has a lot to say about joy, as one would expect:

- "Joy is the feeling that comes from the fulfillment of one's potential" (p. 17).
- "Joy requires a vital, alive body, self-contentment, productive and satisfying relations with others, and a successful relation to society" (p. 17).
- "... Our needs from and toward other people are three: inclusion, control, and affection. We achieve interpersonal joy when we find a satisfying, flexible balance in each of these areas between ourselves and other people." (pp. 21-22).
- "Joy at the level of organization comes when society and culture are supporting and enhancing to self-realization" (p, 22)
- "How is joy attained? A large part of the effort, unfortunately, must go into undoing. Guilt, shame, embarrassment, or fear of punishment, failure, success, retribution—all must be overcome. Obstacles to release must be surmounted. Destructive and blocking behavior, thoughts, and feelings must be altered. Talents and abilities must be developed and trained" (p. 23).

It is at this point that encounter groups (or T-groups as they came to be known) came into the picture. It was in these groups of six to twelve people that individuals worked at attaining the kind of growth that brought joy. The goal of the group was personal growth. The agenda was not preset but emerged from the group itself under the guidance of its skilled leader. A variety of physical and verbal exercises were undertaken to effect the desired end. In the 60's organizations flourished through which such "sensitivity training" could be undertaken. Schutz himself was connected with the Esalen Institute in Big Sur, California.

And so "joy" entered our vocabulary and our consciousness. We began searching for joy. We left that which limited joy (even if it was spouse, family, or career). We read books with titles like *The Joy of Cooking, The Joy of Natural Childbirth,* not to mention *The Joy of Sex.* And we have witnessed the emergence of Yuppies. Yuppies, perhaps as much as any group, typify how the search for joy becomes a way of life. Yuppies are successful, affluent, and committed to a lifestyle that is self-fulfilling and hence, which brings joy. They have the right car, the right condo, the right pasta maker. They eat the right food, drink the right wine, and vacation in the right places. In other words, they typify what has become the national vision of "the good life." No matter that these ex-Hippies (grown older and entered into main-stream America) are themselves an image that does not really exist—at least not in pure form. It is enough that they stand for what we have come to know as the "good life." And the "good life" in turn is how we have come to conceive of joy. I suspect St. Paul might find all this a bit amazing.

UNIT 2—Thanksgiving and Prayer/Philippians 1:3-11

Ready

You survived your first session as a teacher! Congratulations. Hopefully it was a good experience for you. Be assured that it will get easier and easier as the weeks go by to teach Philippians. Beginning is the hard part.

By now you have also begun to develop a "feel" for the book of Philippians: what it is all about, where it is going, how it is constructed. Your familiarity with Philippians will continue to grow as you immerse yourself in it during the coming weeks. At this point in your study, however, it should be clear to you that this is a very personal book. Paul is writing almost a love letter to these folks. By today's standards, he is curiously unrestrained in his expression of affection for them. His warmth is upfront and overflowing. Who said that Paul is a harsh, ascetic, rigid authoritarian? You can put away those false stereotypes forever. In their place, I hope you come to see Paul as the lover—the lover of people and the lover of God.

Of course, a book as personal as Philippians makes special demands on you as teacher. You cannot effectively teach this particular epistle if you remain the aloof academic who dispenses theological wisdom extracted by painstaking study from this piece of biblical literature. Philippians demands that you be as personal and as relational as Paul is here. This is not always easy to do. It is much safer to be the "teacher." Then you do not have to reveal yourself. You reveal only your knowledge. But in so doing you will fail to communicate the pulse of this particular book.

So in the coming weeks you must try to be especially open as you teach Philippians. This means that you need to be sensitive to how you are responding to Philippians on a personal level as you study it. What does it make you feel? How does it impact on who you are as a person? What light does it shed on your past experience and your current situation?

For example, recall the past week in light of Philippians 1:3-11. Who were your "partners in ministry?" Who assisted you (or who did you assist) in the work of God's kingdom this week—whatever that work was, big or small? How do you feel about these "partners"? Have you been able to express your affection for them as Paul does here? Or is this a point of failure for you? What does all this say, in general, about your relational life? And what about your prayers for these and others? What does Paul's prayer in this section teach you about praying for others? In other words, try to listen to Philippians through the grid of your own experience. And then, be willing to share in class what you discover about yourself and your situation.

You will, of course, have ample opportunity to share this sort of personal insight. As you noticed in last week's session, a certain amount of the discussion revolved around personal experience. The same will be true this week and in subsequent weeks. When you ask these kinds of questions in class, your job as teacher is to be just a little more open than others. Generally, you will want to be the first one to respond to experience-oriented questions. In other words, you ask the question and then you answer it first. In this way you model the kind of response that is appropriate, on-target, and brief enough to allow others to share. Furthermore, in your responses be willing to risk letting people know who you are. Be vulnerable. This will allow others to be open and honest.

Don't let this suggestion scare you, however. You are not being asked to confess all the bad experiences you have had and the evil things you have done. That is just as inappropriate as hiding behind a mask. No, every study group will have its own level of openness. What you want to do is to try to expand this openness by being just a little more honest than the others have been up to that point. They will then follow your lead. Of course, there is a reward for all this. Such openness brings growth to you personally and to the class as a whole. And it brings a response of love and affection from others. This is one of the joys of teaching.

Aim

☐ To discuss the outline of 1:3-11 . . . and so to give a feel for how Paul's thoughts unfold as he writes.

☐ To discuss the anatomy of fellowship . . . and so grasp what Paul teaches about it and how his ideas apply to our current situation.

☐ To reflect on the nature of affection . . . and so understand better what it means to be connected with people.

☐ To reflect on the nature of prayer . . . and so understand better how to pray for others.

Fire

Begin this session by saying: "The unit you studied this past week is typical of what you are going to find in Philippians. It is a mixture—of ideas and feelings, of perceptive insights into the gospel and homey details about Paul's life and experience. It is prayer and theology and affection all jumbled together. And beneath the surface, there flows a keen perception about people and how God meets them. Since this unit is typical of how Philippians is written, let's try to unpack it a bit so that we understand better how Paul writes.

"First of all, a word about structure, that is, about how Paul composed this letter. Now, I

Handwritten notes at top:

① Read Phil 1:3-11
② Read circle ②
③ Discuss circle ③
  a. Talk about Johnsons
  b. Make connection to Lamb of God

④ Discuss Fellowship
  A. Koinonia
  b. Thankfulness - In what ways are we thankful for each other? Specifically, each other in this class.
  c. Insight - they know each other

---

don't think that Paul sat down and did what our sixth-grade English teachers tell us to do, that is, make an outline and then use it to write the essay. He just wrote. One idea suggested another idea, and so the letter unfolded itself. This is not to say that Philippians does not have a coherent structure. It does. Paul's mind is such that it naturally puts things together in meaningful ways. My own sense is that he is incapable of writing incoherently. The problem is that his implicit structure is not always evident to the casual reader. We have to work with a passage for a while until it reveals how it is put together.

"All this is to say that in 1:3-11, there is structure. Paul's thoughts can be outlined. This is what we want to look at: how 1:3-11 unfolds. The first thing to note is that the format of a Greek letter provides the focus for what Paul says in this unit. *[② begin]* After the salutation in a letter, it is typical to offer a prayer in honor of the recipients of the letter. This is what Paul does here. He offers thanks to God for what good friends and colleagues the Philippians have been. As he says this, he gets in touch with all the affection he has for them. So he tells them how much he cares for them. His affection, in turn, leads to prayer. How else could he express such feelings sitting there in a prison, far away from all of them? So he tells them what he is praying, and thus the unit ends.

"Do you see how this unit unfolds? Thanks leads to affection which leads to prayer. [You might want to put these three terms up on the chalkboard.] There is a coherent flow to the ideas. This is what we must be searching for constantly in all Bible study: the flow of the author's thoughts.

"But there is something else happening here simultaneously. What we have been talking about so far is the surface structure—Paul's thoughts move from thanks to affection to prayer. But beneath this movement of thought, ③ there is in Paul's mind an image of the Philippians: who they are, what his relationship to them is, and where they are in their Christian life. And it is this image of the people to whom he is writing that governs what he says by way of thanks, affection, and prayer. Who are the Philippians and where are they in their Christian life? How are they bound to Paul and why? What are their needs? In other words, why does Paul write as he does here in verses 3-11? It is by probing at this level that we get some of the best insights into what Paul is trying to express.

"This is what I want to do now. I want to look at the realities that underlie what Paul writes. First we want to look at the relationship between Paul and the Philippians as expressed here. By so doing we will come to understand what I call the *anatomy of fellowship*. Then we will look at two key aspects of fellowship: affection and prayer. Let me begin by taking the next few moments to point out some of what Paul says in this passage about fellowship, and then we will discuss it."

Discuss

On Fellowship

Begin your analysis of the passage by presenting the following mini-lecture. You can read the lecture as it is written or you can put this material into your own words. The points to make are listed below. As you lecture, put the words in bold type on the chalkboard, one at a time, as you come to each new point. This will help the class follow what you are saying.

1. Koinonia: "This is a familiar word to most of us—one of the few Greek words we know. Paul uses this word twice in this passage though it is hidden from us because of the way it has been translated. In one instance it is rendered as partnership (1:5) and in the other as 'share' (1:7). These are good translations since they capture what *koinonia* is all about: sharing together in a common venture. By this word Paul refers to the fact that the Philippians have been consistent and faithful supporters of his ministry, often sending financial gifts to him, and assisting him in a variety of ways. So, real fellowship involves more than just going to a church supper once a month. It involves partnership in a common venture that has kingdom value.

2. Thankfulness: "This kind of sharing, in good times and bad, brings with it a sense of thankfulness for others. Thankfulness is the first fruit of fellowship. Paul needed the Philippians and they needed him. They were grateful for each other. Paul expresses his gratitude in 1:3-6. [Read these verses aloud.] He expresses his thankfulness both to God and to them. He is grateful for what they have done to support him and he is grateful to God who inspired this active support on their part. True fellowship, therefore, brings mutual gratitude. If there is no sense of how much we need others, then the depth of our fellowship is suspect.

3. Affection: "A second fruit of fellowship is affection. Paul really likes these folks. They are not just anonymous donors who get his prayer letter each month. He cares for them. He wants to be with them. And he tells them so. The affection he feels for them is connected to the affection that Christ has for all his children. (Read verses 7-8 aloud.) True fellowship, then, brings love for others which issues in warm feelings and the active bearing of each other's burdens. Notice too, how openly and freely Paul expresses his affection. He is not the cold, calculating stoic we sometimes picture him as.

4. Insight: "A third fruit of fellowship is insight. We come to know the real needs of those we are in fellowship with. We thus understand how to pray for them. Notice how specific Paul's prayer for the Philippians is. He knows their situation and their need. (Read verses 9-11 aloud.) Paul's main wish for them is that they will grow in love. They do love, but they need to grow more in love. (Notice: this is exactly what they need if they are to overcome the crisis of disunity which they are facing. Paul does not condemn them by saying they are not loving enough. Instead, he affirms the love that does authenically exist and asks that they be given even more of it.)

"But this is not uninformed love they need. They are facing not only disunity but false teachers who seek to draw them away from basic Christianity. They need to love but not uncritically. They must be able to *discern* what will lead to wholeness—which Paul defines here as purity, blamelessness, and goodness.

"In other words, true fellowship results in accurate insight into the needs each has. Paul prays for their needs at that moment, confident that God will supply the discerning love that is vital to them. And the Philippians knowing of Paul's financial needs, send him a gift (as well as praying for him—1:19). 'Partnership' involves mutual prayer for and support of one another.

"Notice what we have here in verses 3-11: a picture of what the ideal Christian community is all about. This should serve us as a model for what our church ought to look like and as goal for what we want our small group to become."

After this mini-lecture, discuss the ideas which you have presented:

Ask: What else did you learn about fellowship from this passage?

Ask: What have been your most memorable experiences of fellowship? What made the fellowship so good?

Ask: What is our church doing at the moment when it comes to the kind of fellowship Paul describes here?

On Affection
The root from which fellowship grows is relationships between people. You can't have fellowship unless you have caring people connected together in warm relationships. In expressing the dynamics of his relationship with the Philippians, Paul provides valuable insights into the nature of all relationships.

Ask: In this passage, what does Paul teach directly and indirectly about relationships? Answers will include:

☐ He quite freely expresses how he feels about them. Good relationships involve the easy expression of affection and gratitude for the other.

☐ There is a connectedness between the Philippians and Paul. In a good relationship, people are involved in practical ways in each other's lives.

☐ Paul needs them. They are essential to him. He wants to be with them. Good relationships cause us to want to be with others.

☐ Good relationships are rooted in the very affection of Jesus Christ for others, expressing itself through us. Good relationships (and hence true fellowship) spring from the shared life of God in Christ.

☐ In good relationships, people are not blind to the faults of others, but this does not diminish affection. Instead it gives rise to practical concern for each other.

Ask: Why is it that most people have trouble expressing affection? How well do you do in expressing affection?

Ask: [if there is time and it is appropriate] How would you rate your various relationships in terms of what Paul teaches here?

On Prayer
Ask: What does Paul teach us here about prayer? Answers will include:

☐ His prayer began with *thankfulness* for the Philippians (v. 3).

☐ He prayed for them on a *regular basis* (v. 3).

☐ His prayer also included *intercession* in which he asked God to meet their specific needs (v. 4).

☐ Paul prayed for the Philippians out of a heart filled with *joy* (v. 4).

☐ He prayed with *confidence* that God would complete the good work begun in the Philippians (v. 6).

☐ He prayed that they would grow in *discerning love* and so become the kind of people Christ wanted them to be (v. 9-11).

☐ The end result of his prayer would be *"the glory and praise of God"* (v. 11).

Ask: What can you learn about prayer from Paul's model?

Remind

Homework
Assign for homework all of the units you intend to cover in the next session.

Reminder/Empty Chair
Now is the time to really stress the value of reach-out. The class members should know what the course is all about by now and should be able to attract others by their enthusiasm.

Order more Study Guides by calling Serendipity House TOLL FREE 800-525-9563.

UNIT 3—Paul's Chains Advance the Gospel/Philippians 1:12-18a

Ready

Evangelism—the very word sends chills down the spines of many people—and this includes Christians. Christians don't like the word "evangelism" because they might be called to do it—and such a thing is not quite reputable and/or it is downright frightening. "Not our sort of thing, you know. Besides, we really don't have a clue how it is done." As for people outside the church, they get the willies when they hear the word because, who knows, they might be the target of this evangelizing. And they certainly don't want to be button-holed!

And yet, here in this passage, it is quite clear that Paul is all for evangelism. In fact, this is what makes his stay in prison bearable: the fact that the gospel is advancing. He may be in jail, but this has not retarded the work of evangelism. In fact, it has helped it. As a result, he can rejoice . . . even though it must not have been easy for a man as active as Paul to be locked up. But this is okay, he says, as long as evangelism is taking place. Apparently Paul had a different view of evangelism than many of us do.

And, of course, this is exactly the case. We view evangelism through our experience. We remember when we were kids the pulpit-pounding, finger-pointing revivalists who held forth in old tents down in the park. These same guys are still around, except now they are on radio and television. And they still frighten us. We also recall, now that we are adults, that it is not even safe to go to the shopping mall any more because we might be accosted by a bright-eyed young person who wants to give us a pamphlet and tell us about Jesus. Evangelism—who needs it?

Well, Paul apparently needs it. In fact, he glories in it. He rejoices that it is taking place. He is even willing to be in prison if this is what it takes to motivate the Roman Christians to do it.

Why then the disparity between his view and ours? Part of the answer is that we have allowed ourselves to confuse *method* with *message*. We see people doing things in the name of evangelism which we do not like (perhaps with good reason). And since we don't like their methods (and we may be right in feeling that such methods are counterproductive), we write off the whole enterprise.

But these misguided evangelists are not the only ones with a problem. Haven't we failed as well? For one thing, we have failed to see that their message is our message! And we have failed to see that it is this very message which the whole world so desperately needs to hear. Perhaps our most serious failure is to see that at least *they* are out there trying to present the gospel, no matter how ineptly. How well are we doing at "advancing the gospel"?

You see, at its core evangelism is a message, not a method. It is a message about a Savior who came to seek and to save us when we were lost in bondage to "the world, the flesh, and the Devil" (as Paul put it in one of his letters). *How* that message is communicated is secondary. In fact, Paul uses three different words in this short passage to describe its transmission. *That* it is communicated is the crucial thing.

It is clear, then, that we should be evangelizing. If this passage here in Philippians teaches anything it teaches this. How you actually share this message will depend upon who you want to hear it and the circumstances in which you meet them. You don't have to be offensive. Needless to say, it is far better if you are not! You want people to hear the gospel and not just react to your rudeness.

And by the way, what about all those brothers and sisters out there doing evangelism in a way that offends you? I think Paul has something to say about our attitude to them. You'll find it in verse 18.

A word is necessary about how you will teach this unit. Some choices are needed—unless you have a lot of teaching time available. The problem is that there is too much material here to be covered within the time frame of the ordinary class. As you will see when you look over the unit, there are two emphases in the teaching material—*evangelism* (as the above introduction implies) and *suffering* (as you probe how Paul can rejoice while in prison). Both are important. Both need to be covered. Both are central to the passage. But, you probably won't get to analyze each area thoroughly. The problem is that St. Paul's writing is so rich and so filled with content that it is hard to take it all in!

My suggestion is this. Focus on either *evangelism* or *suffering*. Make your choice around the needs of your class. Then, at the end of the class period, simply summarize briefly the topic you failed to cover. Even better, if you have the freedom to do so, why not schedule two class sessions on this one unit? During one class cover the question of evangelism and in the other, deal with the question of Paul and his hardships. Whatever you decide to do, there will be rewarding interaction. This is a potent passage.

Aim

☐ To probe our stereotypes about evangelism . . . and thus develop a healthier view of this form of ministry.

☐ To think about methods of evangelism . . . and so become aware that there is a variety of acceptable ways to go about this.

☐ To notice which Christian groups we distrust . . . and so learn to rejoice in ministries that are different from our own.

☐ To reflect on how Paul can rejoice while in prison ... and so grasp his way of dealing with suffering and hardship.

Fire

Introduction
Begin this session by saying: "Today we are going to begin by talking about evangelism. Now, I know that you may not like the word 'evangelism,' but I didn't choose the topic, Paul did. This is what the passage is all about: advancing the gospel, speaking the Word of God, preaching Christ. Paul says it in a lot of different ways, but it all adds up to the same thing: evangelism.

"We may not like the idea of evangelism, but Paul certainly does. In fact, it is because his imprisonment has stimulated his Christian brothers and sisters to evangelize that he can rejoice, even though he is in jail.

"Why is it that he seems to like evangelism and we often do not?" [At this point use the material in the READY section to complete this introductory lecture.]

Discuss

Evangelism
Ask: When you hear the word evangelism, what do you think of? Answers will include:

☐ *High pressure.* Someone trying to manipulate you by fear or guilt into a religious decision that you would not otherwise make.

☐ *Loving concern.* A friend whose life has been turned around by Jesus wants you to discover this same reality.

☐ *Sawdust trails.* Revivalists in tents who give protracted altar calls in order to get people to "come forward."

☐ *Gift giving.* "One beggar telling another beggar where to find bread," as Bishop D. T. Niles once put it.

☐ *Fear:* that I am going to have to talk to my neighbor about my faith, because if I don't I will be considered a second-rate Christian, even though I haven't a clue what I am supposed to say.

☐ *Excitement:* at hearing a friend discuss his discovery of the reality of the spiritual life.

Ask: What experiences have you had of doing evangelism or being evangelized? (Obviously, there will be a variety of responses, but try to elicit both positive and negative examples.)

Ask: What can we learn from these experiences about how one should go about evangelism? (You may wish to make this into a mini-lecture, in which case use the "answers" below as the basis for the points you want to make.) Answers will include:

☐ You have got to *care authentically* about the other person in order to share the gospel with integrity.

☐ There is *no one, approved method* of doing evangelism. Whatever communicates and is non-manipulative is legitimate.

☐ Unless you are *intentional* about it, you probably won't do much evangelism.

☐ The best evangelism is not contrived but *reflexive.* It occurs not in meetings but in the course of ordinary conversation.

☐ We need to *know how to talk about faith-realities,* otherwise we will lapse into cliches that others don't understand or into incoherence that does not accurately represent Christ.

☐ People really *do want to hear about Christ* and about spiritual reality. They just don't want to be pressured or conned.

Suffering
Introduce this section by means of the following mini-lecture. If it is possible, make an overhead transparency containing the words that are in italics. This will help the class follow your lecture. Make the following points: "Paul ends this unit with these words: 'And because of this I rejoice' (v. 18). These are quite astonishing words given the fact that he writes these words from prison. He urges joy even though he himself is in a hard place. How can he do this? How is it possible to rejoice under such circumstances? Before we try to answer this question, we need to be quite clear that although Paul may not say much about the conditions of his imprisonment, what he is going through is not pleasant. Consider his circumstances:

☐ *He was confined.* Paul was a very active, energetic—one might even say—'driven' man. He had this burning passion to share with the world—the whole world—the astonishing, unexpected, spectacular news that God invaded this planet as the man Jesus who died for our sins. And yet he was confined to one small space. He was in a rented house in Rome which he could not leave.

☐ *He was anxious.* His trial had dragged on for so long. He had been in custody for years, hauled before one court and then another. But still, there was no verdict, no conclusion. And he was rightly concerned about the outcome of his trial. He is optimistic. He is confident that he will be released. But this is by no means certain. In fact, he is thinking about death. Death has even become desirable to him. What if he is forced to languish in jail for years more? What if he is sentenced to death? What if his imprisonment begins to work against the gospel? Paul was not immune to anxiety.

☐ *He was uncomfortable.* Prison life is not pleasant. It was not intended to be. The food was probably not great. It was undoubtedly boring, confined to a single house. It was inconvenient, chained to an endless number of soldiers. And then, of course, there was his 'thorn in the flesh.' We don't know exactly what this was, but it probably had a physical component to it. If you entered prison unwell physically, you probably would not improve while incarcerated.

"In other words, although Paul does not say much directly about his personal circumstances, it is clear that they were not pleasant and involved suffering. It is interesting to note that Paul says nothing about altering his situation. He accepts being in jail as a given. He does not waste time over something he cannot change. This is not to say that he would not like to be released. He longs to be out of prison and with the Philippians. He wants deliverance. This will become evident in the next unit. But the point is that in the midst of something he cannot change, he has learned to accept it and deal with what is rather than fretting about what should be.

"This brings us back to the issue of joy in the midst of suffering. Paul's situation is not very pleasant. So how can he rejoice? How can he end this section by saying: 'And because of this I rejoice'? What is his secret? How does he do it? I think that we have some hints in this unit that enable us to answer this question. Note:

☐ *He sees his situation in the context of the larger issues involved.* Notice what Paul says about his imprisonment in this report to his friends. His concern is not with his personal problems but with the task he has been given by God. His focus is on the advance of the gospel, not on getting out of prison. In other words, he has learned to see his problems in the context of God's work in the world. He has learned to see what is happening to him through the grid of God's ultimate plan for the world. In this way he is able to move beyond an emphasis on his personal situation to an emphasis on the larger picture. He focuses on God's plan, not on his circumstances.

☐ *He does not focus on his needs but on the needs of others.* What Paul is concerned about is not how comfortable he is, how difficult prison life is for him, or how he might improve his lot. His concern is that other people hear the gospel and so move from the kingdom of darkness into the kingdom of light. He focuses on others, not on himself.

☐ *He has learned to see the good in the midst of the evil.* He is in jail—unfairly—but he does not focus on this injustice. Instead, he focuses on the fact that because he is in jail, a whole circle of people are hearing the gospel who would not otherwise have done so. Some rival Christian groups are trying to stir up trouble for him but he does not focus on their misdeeds. Rather, he focuses on the fact that they are preaching Christ. He comments on the good in the situation, not on the evil."

Ask: What else do you see in this passage that might explain Paul's ability to rejoice in difficult circumstances?

Ask: What kinds of problems do people typically face these days? What causes us to suffer? Answers will include:

☐ *Relational Problems.* Marriages are breaking up, children are getting involved in destructive activity, communities are torn asunder, etc.

☐ *Physical Problems.* Heart attacks, cancer, illness and accidents of various sorts affect us and our loved ones.

☐ *Economic Problems.* There is not enough work, not enough money to pay bills, bad investments, etc.

☐ *Problems of Meaning.* Satisfaction in life is gone, there is no sense of purpose or meaning, our self-image is damaged and distorted, etc.

☐ *Environmental Problems.* The water and air are polluted, the land is blighted, harmful chemicals are in the food chain, etc.

☐ *International Problems.* There is war, discord between tribes and nations, terrorism, hatred, etc.

Ask: What are some of the less successful ways by which we deal with problems? Answers will include:

☐ *Denial.* We pretend that we do not have a problem.

☐ *Wishful thinking.* We live in a fantasy world that shields us from harsh reality.

☐ *Avoidance.* We focus on something else as a way of not admitting there is a problem.

☐ *Flight.* We run away from our problem.

- *Speculation.* We embrace a world view in which problems do not exist (e.g., the Christian Science view that suffering is not real).
- *Anger.* We rail against the source of our problem although this does not in any way alter the situation.
- *Projection.* We blame others for our problems and try to make them responsible.

Ask: How does the perspective which Paul gives in this chapter enable us to cope with problems? Answers will include:

- He focuses on the larger issues and not his personal circumstances. We need to see our circumstances in the context of what God is doing in, through, and around us. We need to remember that in the ultimate sense God has won and we are on his side. Thus we can accept what is and live within that reality in the light of the larger reality of God's ultimate plan.
- He focuses on the needs of others and not on his needs. We need to move our vision off of our difficulties onto the needs of others.
- He focuses on the good and not on the bad. We need to learn to see that which is positive in our difficult situation and not just be overwhelmed by what is negative.
- He rejoices instead of complains. This attitude makes suffering easier to bear.
- (By implication in this passage), his faith in Jesus is the center of his life. When our relationship with Jesus is alive and vital we are energized on an inner level and are thus enabled through his power to cope.

End this discussion by reading the essay in the **Comment** section entitled: "Suffering in the New Age."

Remind

Homework
Look ahead to next week and assign the unit (or units) that you want the class to study.

Reminder/Empty Chair
This is the time you need to be on guard against a complacent attitude in the class—where people will get so excited about their own spiritual growth that they forget about others. Remind each group to remember the challenge to bring new people to the meeting—people who are hungry for spiritual growth and need to belong to a study group.

Comment

Suffering in the New Age
Somehow this one got by us. Suffering is still around despite all our awesome achievements and our New Age philosophy. Ironic, isn't it? We have built satellites to circle the earth, developed reusable rockets to put them up there, and crafted cameras sharp enough to photograph Bedouin caravans trekking across the Sahara from high up in the sky. We have made enough cars so that nearly everyone has one, put a television set in 98% of American homes, and tamed the weather (well, at least tracked the weather. We now know when the storm will happen if not how to stop it from happening).

But suffering—that's still with us. Oh, we've got wonder drugs. (They really are wonderful as you learn when your infant is ill.) And we've got OSHA to help us cut down on accidents. We have child-proof caps on our drugs; we have machines in our hospitals that analyze, digitize, and synthesize miraculous amounts of medical information. And we have courses on stress management. But for all this we still suffer. Suffering continues to hang around no matter what we do. We still get ill. We still get old. We still fall down. We still grow depressed. We still destroy relationships. Even in this New Age, suffering is still here.

So we have a New Age philosophy to help us cope with suffering. It consists of a number of maxims. Like . . . "Health is more than the mere absence of disease." In other words, optimum health goes beyond merely not having a disease or not having a functional disability. Health, in this sense, involves the well-being of the whole organism—body, mind, and spirit. Here is another maxim. "We are responsible for our own health." Good advice. For too long we have given over the authority for our bodies to the medical establishment. How about . . . "New methods of promoting health must be explored." Right. There is acupuncture, biofeedback, body-work therapies, meditation, visualization, and nutritional therapy. All potentially good stuff when properly used.[1]

But even with all this good advice (and it is very useful), accidents still happen; microbes continue to invade our bodies uninvited, and our body chemistry sometimes gets out of whack. We do get sick. What then? Furthermore, even when we are physically well, we can be emotionally sick. Our parents kick us out of the house; we lose a job we love; our car is totaled. All this takes a toll on us. We don't sleep; we grow depressed; we drag ourselves through each day.

Well, maybe it is a matter of mind over matter—or so some New Age philosophers would

---

[1] This paragraph was influenced by the material in chapter 3 of *Unmasking the New Age* by Douglas R. Groothuis, (Downers Grove, IL: InterVarsity Press) 1986.

tell us. What we need is a "change of consciousness." In order to cope with reality when it turns harsh on us, we need to "get our vision straight." We need to "see beyond the traditional metaphors." We need to "get in touch with real reality." In New Age practice this means we need to follow one of several non-traditional paths into a new consciousness. Classical Eastern religions will do—Buddhism, Taoism, Hinduism, especially in their modern forms. Or perhaps it is the way of the shaman we need to follow—as described by Michael Harper or Carlos Castaneda. If not sorcery, then one of the Self-Development paths will do—the martial arts, esalen, est ("The Forum" as it is now called). There is always the occult to explore (witchcraft is on the rise). Or pyramid power, sensory-deprivation tanks, or out-of-body experiences. The path doesn't matter as long as it gets us beyond the suffering.

But does it? Isn't this just Christian Science *revividus?* Pretend it doesn't exist and it is not there. Change our attitude and change our suffering? Now, attitude is important. St. Paul's attitude was crucial in helping him deal with his suffering. But it was not "attitude" alone that made the difference for Paul. It was his faith. And here I am not speaking about "faith" as if it too were mere "attitude." No, it was the *content of his faith* that made the difference. And the content of his faith can be summed up in one word: Jesus. The one irreducible *given* that made all the difference for Paul was Jesus Christ. Paul had met Christ on the road to Damascus. (Or was it Christ who had encountered Paul?) And his life was transformed. It was Jesus who gave Paul this new vision. It was Jesus who brought about his new attitudes. It was his faith in and obedience to Jesus that made all the difference. It is that simple. The root of Paul's joy in the midst of suffering is the love of Jesus Christ. He was "in Christ" and Christ was "in him"—as he never tired of saying in his letters.

Don't get me wrong. I am not automatically anti anything that is tinged with the New Age label. To be sure, when New Age thought is seen as a system which is complete in itself—a world view that purports to reveal the mysteries of the universe—then it does stand in opposition to historic Christianity. But, still, there are good elements within the rather broad, fuzzy area we call New Age. However, it is also quite clear that while New Age thought has some interesting things to say about suffering, ultimately it fails. It fails because Jesus is not perceived to be the center of reality. In the end, joy in the midst of hardship is derived from the sure knowledge that Jesus is there with you in the midst of the suffering and that he will continue to be with you, both now and forever. There is no way to rid this world of suffering despite our technology and philosophy, but Jesus helps us cope with the way this world is (and that is not just a pious cliche, folks). He is with us in the here and now. And he is with us in the Future. He is with us in the New Age. In fact, he is himself inaugurating the New Age. And in the New Age that Jesus will bring to pass "there will be no more death or mourning or crying or pain, for the old order of things has passed away." All this will take place because God will then dwell with men and women. "He will live with them. They will be his people, and God himself will be with them and be their God" (Rev. 21:3-4). This is the ultimate New Age answer to suffering.

Rom 6:23
1 Cor 15:54
Rev 21
Ps 116:15

UNIT 4—Life or Death?/Philippians 1:18b-26

Ready

How did you do with evangelism? It is one thing to discuss joy or fellowship or relationships (as you did in Units 1 and 2). It is another to discuss a subject that is potentially as controversial as evangelism. People have such rigid stereotypes about evangelism. Depending upon your denominational affiliation, evangelism is either the in-thing to do or the out-thing not to do. In some churches, being interested in evangelism certifies you as a committed, "on-fire" Christian. While in other churches, it certifies you as a nut. In other words, evangelism is the kind of subject about which there are strong views. Teaching a lesson on the subject can be very interesting!

Well, if you had trouble with the last session, cheer up. In this session you get to tackle not one, but two controversial topics! In this unit the subjects are death and emotions. However, the problem with teaching these topics is the opposite from teaching about evangelism. With evangelism, it is usually very easy to get people to express their strong views. With these two topics the problem is getting people to say anything. It is curious, but in our culture both of these are subjects about which we have little to say—despite our deep feelings. We don't talk about death and we don't express emotions. At least not publicly. But here in this unit, Paul does both. He ruminates about his own death and he does so in the context of strong feelings.

These topics are alike in one way, however. In the same way that we need to be liberated from our fear of evangelism, we also need to be liberated from our fear of death and our fear of emotions. When it comes to each of these areas, Paul is for us a model of what we want to become. He is a passionate, committed evangelist—*because* he has experienced the life-changing power of Jesus. He is a true friend who cares deeply for others and is not afraid to say so—*because* Christ has made them his brothers and sisters. He is a man who can rather wistfully long for death—*because* he has experienced union with Christ and thus looks forward eagerly to a reunion with the Lord. In other words, his attitude in regard to evangelism, to death, and to emotional expression is forged out of his experience of Christ.

Well, by now it should be clear to you that Philippians is not quite the innocuous letter that it first appeared to be—safe and soothing to study because Paul doesn't get into controversial subjects here! Another stereotype bites the dust.

As far as teaching this material: let it be what it is without apology. You don't have to defend Paul or skirt the subjects he raises. Let the text speak for itself and then create the kind of comfortable climate that will allow you to explore this material without hesitation. By the way, about teaching controversial topics: it really isn't harder to tackle these. If anything, it is more fun because you know (1) the discussion will be lively and (2) the learning will be significant. Both add up to a good teaching/learning experience.

Aim

☐ To examine Paul's views of life and death . . . and so discover the centrality of Christ in both.

☐ To reflect on our cultural and personal views of death . . . and to see how Paul's perspective defuses fear and gives perspective.

☐ To note the emotional quality of this passage . . . and to learn about our own way of expressing emotion.

Fire

Begin this session by saying: "Today we are going to talk about life and death. Once again, Paul forces us to examine an area that we would probably rather avoid. In the last session, you might have been saying to yourself: Who wants to talk about evangelism? Today, I know some of you are feeling: Who wants to talk about death?

"Still, these are the very issues we ought to be facing. If evangelism makes us feel uncomfortable, then we need to analyze why. If the topic of death creates anxiety, then we need to face the source of our fear and deal with it. The Christian life is like this. Our growth comes at those points where we feel uncomfortable. It is here, at the cutting edge of our life, that the Holy Spirit is at work.

"Death. Evangelism. Both topics are connected, you know. Death holds little terror for Paul precisely because in the gospel he finds the kind of hope that mutes the terror of dying. You see, this is what the gospel is all about: a Savior who is so strong that his love holds on to us even beyond the grave. This is what Paul went around Europe and Asia Minor preaching. 'Jesus is alive and powerful and he loves you. Come, meet him, open your life to him,' Paul would urge. 'Commit your life to him. Be his person. Follow him.' This was his message. This was his passion. People needed to hear this. They no longer had to live with the terror of the grave. Beyond the grave there was Jesus who loved them.

"Of course, this same Jesus whom Paul knew so well is still alive and active today. We know him. His love still reaches out to us. Thus the terror of death need not overwhelm us either. But, of course, this is far easier said than felt. Death is not something that is easy to face, even as a Christian. This is why we need to listen to Paul in this passage. There is here in this unit the kind of perspective that can have a deep impact on us."

Discuss

Living and Dying
"It is not possible to discuss Paul's view of death without first discussing his view of life. The two are intimately connected. How he lived determined how he viewed death."

Ask: What does Paul say in this passage about living? Answers will include:

- No matter what Paul does (live or die), he wants Jesus to be displayed to the world in all his greatness (v. 20).
- The center of life is Christ (v. 21).
- The point of life is fruitful labor for Christ (v. 22).
- True life involves a deep commitment to the welfare of one's friends (vv. 23-26).
- Such involvement with others has joy as its aim: bringing to them "joy in the faith" and "joy in Jesus" (vv. 25-26).

Ask: What does Paul say in the passage about death? Answers will include:

- No matter what Paul does (live or die), he wants Jesus to be exalted (v. 20).
- Dying would be of value to him—"a gain" (v. 21).
- He does not know what he would choose (if he were given the option): to go on living (so he can labor fruitfully) or to die (and so be with Christ).
- To die is to be with Christ, then and there, face to face—and this is the best of all.

Ask: How do Paul's views of life relate to his views of death? Answers will include:

- At the center of both stands Jesus. To live is Jesus. To die is Jesus.
- Paul's union with Jesus in life is that which prepares him for his union with Jesus in death.
- Death will bring no substantial change for Paul, except that now he will know Jesus in fullness, face to face.
- By implication, the anticipation of this reunion with Jesus on the other side of death, makes it possible to bear life with its many hardships.

In other words, Paul views death the way he views life: it is being with Jesus. This is the point you want to stress. Paul can feel comfortable with death because for him at the center of both life and death is Jesus. Is it not true that we often feel uncomfortable with death, because for us Jesus is at the periphery of our lives. We lack that keen desire to be with Jesus that gives Paul his perspective. It is as we make Jesus the center of our lives that we lose our terror of death. It is that simple and that hard. Keep this in mind as you probe now both cultural and personal views of death.

Ask: How do Paul's views contrast with contemporary American views? Answers will include:

- There is a terror of death on the part of many contemporary Americans.
- Thus, we avoid the topic of death. (It has been said that for our Victorian forebearers, sex was a taboo subject while death was freely discussed, but in the twentieth century, we have reversed the two. Death is considered obscene while sexuality is omnipresent.)
- For us, this life is all there is, so we have become materialists grabbing all we can get because once we die, we assume it is all over. (For Paul, life was all about fruitful labor for Christ.)
- Without faith in Christ, we cannot afford to face death. We have no perspective that will pull its sting.
- Death is still a terror because of the uncertainty about what really is on the other side.
- We fear the physical pain of dying.
- The loss of all that makes one unique—family, friends, creativity, the power to taste and smell and see, the experience of this planet itself, etc.—make death a great threat. We see nothing beyond this life that we can imagine could be better.
- Having majored in materialism and minored in Jesus, we are uneasy about the future.

Read aloud the article in the **Comment** section entitled: "On Death and Dying in the New Age."

Ask: How do these views match up with those held by people you know—or, perhaps by you yourself?

Ask: How can we begin to shed the terror that the thought of death brings to us? Answers will include:

- By making Jesus the true center of our existence.
- By developing our relationship with him so that we know him well enough in life that we will long to meet him in death.
- By truly believing that at death, we do meet Jesus then and there.

Ask: How do these views of life and death relate to our interest in and effectiveness at evangelism? Answers will include:

- When Jesus is at the center of our lives, we cannot help but share him with others.
- Our hesitation to evangelize is often a hesitation bred out of uncertainty about our faith.
- When we see the terror that death holds for others, we cannot help but share the fact that Jesus overcame death and that he promises that we as his brothers and sisters will do the same.
- Our experience of Jesus—in life and as we face the reality of death—is our strongest motivation to evangelism.

Emotions

Shift the topic now to a related subject: Paul's willingness to share his feelings freely with his friends.

Ask: Scan this passage. Identify all the words and phrases that express emotion or relate to how Paul is feeling. Answers will include:

- Rejoice (v. 18b), joy (vv. 25-26).
- I eagerly expect and hope (v. 20).
- Ashamed/courage (v. 20).
- Exalted (v. 20).
- What shall I choose? (v. 22).
- I am torn (v. 23).
- I desire (v. 23).
- Better by far (v. 23).
- Overflow (v. 26).

Ask: How does this free expression of emotion by Paul compare or contrast with your own expression of feelings? Answers will include:

- People vary in their ability to note and name emotion.
- Many of us are afraid to express strong feelings.
- Sometimes we can express negative emotions (anger, fear) but not positive emotions (love, joy); or vice versa.
- Some people are simply not in touch with the emotional side of life on any but the most superficial level.
- We sometimes feel that strong displays of emotion are out of place in a church context.

Ask: What did you learn from Paul about the emotional side of life?

Remind

Homework
Assign all of the unit or units for homework that you intend to cover next week.

Reminder/Empty Chair
Remind the class of the symbol of the empty chair for the person they should invite next week. Order more Study Guides if you are out.

Comment

On Death and Dying in the New Age

About one-quarter of a million people will die today. The same number will die tomorrow. And the same number the day after that. Day in and day out, people will continue to die. The number of people who die each day will not diminish either. As our population grows, so too will the number of deaths. Death is the most certain reality on our planet. It is omnipresent. It is inevitable. We must all experience it. Death is the price we pay for living.

Not surprisingly, death—and especially life after death—has been a topic of interest from antiquity down to our own day. Prehistoric people reflected on what happens when we die. One scholar notes: "We are told of 'unmistakable indications of a conception of the continuance of life after death' as long as half a million years ago, found in caves near Peking."[1] The Greek myths, the Egyptian *Book of the Dead,* the Mexican celebration of the Day of the Dead, the Vedantic theory of reincarnation all witness to our struggle to make sense out of dying and what follows.

In recent years in the English-speaking world, several new movements have emerged that seek to understand and confront the experience of dying. One involves the insights of Elisabeth Kübler-Ross in the United States by which we have come to understand the stages of dying. Another revolves around the work of Cecily Saunders in England and the Hospice movement which seeks to make the process of dying comfortable and humane.

Probably the most significant of these new movements emerges from the work of Raymond Moody and his investigation into what have been called "near-death experiences" (NDE's in the jargon). Moody, a medical doctor, became fascinated with the reports of those who were clinically "dead" but then after a few moments (or even up to twenty minutes later) "revived." These people then told of such things as traveling down a dark tunnel, of meeting dead friends and relatives who welcomed them into what happened to be a new realm of reality, of encountering a "being of light," of the wrench of being "brought

---
[1] p. 55, *Death and Eternal Life,* John Hick (London: The MacMillan Press), 1976, 1985.

back" to space-time reality. Kenneth Ring, in his best-selling book *Heading Toward Omega,* calls such experiences an "interior view of death" which he says must be set alongside the traditional view of death which is "from the outside." What we learn from those who had a near-death experience, Ring says, is that death is not the terror we thought it to be. We viewed it from the outside as spectators and found it to be terrifying. They viewed death from inside and found it to be pleasant, even ecstatic. In a NDE one has the sense of being made completely whole and of being "engulfed in an ocean of perfect and total love."[2] Furthermore, once a person has gone through a NDE that person forever loses the fear of death.

Fascinating stuff. Do NDE's "prove" the existence of an afterlife? Do they demonstrate that all is well for all who die? Do they negate the claims of various religious groups as to how one achieves life after death? Certainly there is the aura of a religion about what the near-death experience has become for many. Ring views it as "the leading edge" of a new "evolutionary wave."

As Ring says, "I believe and argue in this book *Heading Toward Omega* that humanity as a whole is collectively struggling to awaken to a new and higher mode of consciousness, which many have already called 'planetary consciousness.' Furthermore, I believe that a significant number of persons have already evolved or are evolving toward that form of consciousness and that the NDE can be viewed as an evolutionary device to bring about this transformation, over a period of years, in millions of persons."[3] This is a strong "faith statement" and characteristic of New Age thought. Ring candidly admits that in writing *Heading Toward Omega,*"I am not writing a book dealing mainly with empirical matters to be decided by reference to the canons of scientific inquiry. There are data, to be sure, in this book, but I will be mainly concerned with their *meaning*.... The reader must be prepared to consider issues that science alone is not equipped to resolve."[4]

In fact, when one looks closely at what Ring and others call NDE's, they begin to look suspiciously like another category of experience, namely, mystical experiences. (Ring, himself, makes this connection.) In other words, a near-death experience seems to be one of many "triggers" that promote a mystical experience. This helps give us some perspective on what NDE's mean and do not mean. For one thing, there is a real question as to whether they say anything specific about death, *per se,* or simply point toward the reality of the supernatural and the ability of human beings to experience it in direct ways. (John Hick comments: "Since the patients have proved capable of being resuscitated, we know that they were not completely dead."[5]) For another thing, while NDE's often seem to evoke a new spirituality in people, they are not equivalent to a conversion experience. Conversion experiences are distinct from mystical experiences. A mystical experience can lead to a conversion response but does not necessarily or invariably do so. A mystical experience may awaken one to the reality and personhood of God but it takes submission to that God via repentance and faith in Jesus to bring about the total life reorientation we call Christian conversion.

And this is the point. Mystical experiences are surprisingly common. (One estimate, based on research, is that 35% of adult Americans have had what can only be called mystical experiences.[6] NDE's are one form of mystical experience which George Gallup, Jr. estimates 5 percent of our adult population to have had.[7]) But they need to be "responded to" in order for the reality they represent to become a part of one's life.

Back to death. What does Jesus say about life after death and how to achieve it? In fact, it is quite clear that "the afterlife was taken for granted by Jesus and by his hearers generally. He did not need to impress it or correct it. It was not for him or them a question of hesitation or debate. It is therefore an assured ingredient of his perspective."[8] And, of course, it was Jesus' own resurrection from the dead that pointed out the way to God. In his resurrection he became the forerunner of what his followers would experience: resurrection to life everlasting.

It is this resurrection life that is so appealing to Paul. For Paul, to be with Jesus was so wonderful. Paul's whole life was built around knowing Jesus. Death was the pathway to the fullness of this knowledge. And yet, as Paul says almost with a sigh, it is probably more important that he remain with them all. But, one day, face to face, in wholeness, bathed in light and love ... one day he will stand before Jesus whom he had loved for so long. This is real life after death.

---

[2]Ring, p. 20.
[3]p. 7
[4]p. 30
[5]*Ibid.*, p. 10.
[6]p. 140, *Ecstasy: A Way of Knowing*, Andrew Greeley (Englewood Cliffs, NJ: Prentice-Hall, Inc.) 1974.
[7]*Adventures in Immortality,* (New York: McGraw-Hill), 1982.
[8]pp. 139-140, "Intimations of Immortality in the Thought of Jesus," by Henry J. Cadbury in *Immortality and Resurrection*, ed. Krister Stendahl (New York: MacMillan) 1965.

UNIT 5—Living Worthy of the Gospel/Philippians 1:27-2:4

Ready

Paul begins this letter by discussing his own situation, but it does not take him very long to get to the problems faced by the Philippians. This is quite characteristic of Paul. He may talk about himself when necessary, but his real concern is for others. This is where Paul's heart is. One gets the sense that he considers his own situation trivial. He is quite willing to be poured out as a libation on behalf of others if necessary (2:17). It is no big deal if he has to endure suffering—as long as the word gets out that Jesus is alive, so that the lives of hurting men and women can be changed. Paul really is an other-oriented person.

And, of course, this is what he talks about here in this passage: being a person for others. He needs to encourage the Philippians to relate to one another in this way since, apparently, there is a certain amount of tension between people which has resulted in disunity. Paul knows why there is disunity in the Philippian church. It has to do with ego, with pride, with standing on rights, with demanding rights. It has to do with not being humble. Disunity is created in a church when "selfish ambition," "vain conceit," or "not looking out for the interests of others" prevails.

Disunity is always a problem when it occurs in the church, but for the Philippians it had especially serious consequences. Unless they could get their act together inside the church, they were never going to be able to cope with the pressures that are coming at them from outside the church.

It is interesting to note that Paul tackles this problem of disunity indirectly. He doesn't say: "You've got a problem. You are not united. You've got to do something about this!" Instead, he focuses on the outside pressure and says that unity is the way to combat this. In other words, he focuses on a problem which they perceive so that he can get them to face a problem they are blind to. By not confronting them directly over the issue of disunity, he gives them the space to see the problem and deal with it. Direct confrontation could cause them to be defensive, making it harder for them to admit that anything is wrong. Sometimes the indirect approach is best. (At other times, direct confrontation may be what is called for. Paul is certainly not reticent to confront people as Peter, the Judaizers, and the Corinthians all knew!)

The Philippians are not alone in this problem of pride, of course. There is within each of us this same very human impulse that looks out for number one, even if it is at the price of others. Christians are no different from anyone else when it comes to self-centeredness. The same issue of pride confronts us as it did the Philippians. Yet what is different about Christians, hopefully, is that we know about our tendency toward self-centeredness and are fighting against it.

So, your challenge today as teacher is to help the class see the spiritual principles involved in the problem in Philippi (disunity due to self-centeredness), to help them see this same problem in themselves, and to help them see Paul's antidote to pride (humility). Along the way, you will also look at Paul's rather intriguing suggestion that suffering is the norm for the Christian and by it we somehow enter into Christ's own work of bearing the suffering of the world.

Aim

☐ To understand the two-fold problem of the Philippians (pressure from without from false teachers and pressure from within from disunity) . . . and so come to understand better these same issues in our own lives.

☐ To confront the question of suffering in the life of the Christian . . . and so grasp how we can enter into Christ's own work of bearing the suffering of the world.

☐ To identify the several faces of pride . . . and then see how to develop humility instead.

Fire

Begin by saying: "As you know by now, in this unit Paul shifts his focus. Up to this point he had been discussing his own situation. But here he looks at the situation faced by the Philippians. And in light of what he sees, he has one major thing to say: 'You have got to work on developing a harmonious fellowship.' He sees a church which is no longer unified and he knows that unless they recover their sense of oneness in Christ, they will fall prey to the false teachers who are holding forth in their area. Without a sense of unity, they will be like frightened horses that stampede off in all directions at the least sign of danger.

"So, from 1:27 down to 2:18, Paul describes how the Philippians can develop unity in their church. It is really very simple. The formula by which unity is achieved is not at all complex. All the Philippians have to do is to become humble servants concerned about the needs of others. Unity will then emerge automatically. Unity is a by-product of humility.

"Of course, this is the rub. None of us is very good at humility. In fact, we are very bad when it comes to humility. And as for looking out for the interests of others, we'd far prefer to look out for our own interests, thank you! With this being the case, it is important for all of us to listen with some care to what Paul has to say, because he is touching upon the kind of issues that can make us very resistant. We don't like to face and own our self-interest. So, let's pray as we begin this lesson that the Lord will give us unusual insight into our own complex motivations, both in terms of how we relate within this church and how we relate to our family and friends.

"Let's pray: 'Lord Jesus, open our hearts and minds today that we may hear with clarity your word of truth. Help each of us to identify those areas in our own lives where self-interest tends to prevail. And then, in coming to see our sin, may we simultaneously see your grace which forgives and your powerful love which heals. We pray this in your name. Amen.'"

Discuss

Sharing in Suffering

Continue your mini-lecture: "Paul does not confront this problem of disunity directly. He eases into it by focusing on the problem they are having with false teachers. He says, in essence, that the only way to cope with the false teachers is by presenting a unified front. Once he has defined the problem in this way, then he can go on to share with the Philippians how such unity can be achieved.

"This is an interesting approach on Paul's part. Were he to have hit them head on by saying: 'Look gang, you've got to get your act together. You are not unified,' he would have run the risk of creating defensiveness on their part. And you know what it is like when people are defensive. They don't hear a word you say. You may have life-saving advice for them, but they are so busy defending themselves, they seem literally unable to grasp what you are trying to communicate. But since Paul has put his advice in terms of the felt needs of the Philippians, they can and will listen to him.

"Let's begin by examining the first paragraph in this unit. In the course of defining the problem Paul also offers us a fascinating glimpse into the nature and meaning of suffering.

Ask: What is the situation faced by the Philippians? What words and phrases does Paul use in 1:27-30 to define the problem? Answers will include:

- They must make sure they *conduct themselves in a manner worthy of the gospel.* By this Paul implies that they are in a situation in which they might be tempted to act in unchristian ways (v. 27).
- They need to act in this way *whether or not Paul is there.* They must be inner motivated and not just live like good Christians when an authority figure is present (v. 27).
- They need to *stand firm in one spirit.* Paul pictures them as if they were soldiers fighting valiantly together against a common foe (v. 27).
- They need to *contend as one man.* Paul pictures them as if they were athletes on the same team, striving toward the same goal (v. 27).
- That which is in *jeopardy* is the belief system and lifestyle which emerges from the gospel (v. 27).
- There is a possibility that they can be so badly *frightened* that they will bolt from their faith like horses that have been shied (v. 28).
- They face an unnamed set of foes who *oppose* them (v. 28).
- Those foes think that the persecution the Philippian church is facing will lead to its destruction, but the Philippians know it will lead to their salvation (v. 28b).
- Such suffering is, in fact, a gift of grace (v. 29).
- Their suffering parallels that of Paul's (v. 30).

Summarize these findings by making the following points:

- There are two problems faced by the Philippian church: pressure from without by false teachers and pressure from within by reason of disunity.
- Paul directly states the first problem (external opposition) but only implies the second (inner unity). (He urges unity, which would be unnecessary if they were already unified.)
- The problems are serious and require direct action on the part of the Philippians.
- The pressure they are feeling is not unusual for Christians. It is one way they participate in the work of Christ in the world.

Ask: In what ways are Christians suffering today around the world? Answers will include:

- In some places, Christians are put to death because of their faith (e.g., in Central America).
- In other places, Christians are put in jail because of actions arising out of their faith—even in America (e.g., those jailed for helping Latin American immigrants or for opposing nuclear arms).
- By acting ethically, some Christians are hurt financially.
- In certain situations, a Christian world view brings scorn and rejection.

Ask: What does it mean in your own situation to "suffer for him (Christ)"? There will be a wide range of answers drawn from personal experience, including:

- As Christ's people, we are called to enter into the suffering of others (the distraught, the lonely, the hungry, the dying, those with broken homes, etc.) and to share their burdens in Christ's name.

- We live with openness to suffering—both that due to disaster and that due to injustice—and work toward its alleviation.
- We feel the pain of the world when we see it through Christ's eyes.
- We face pain instead of denying it or running from it.

The Four Faces of Self-Centeredness
Ask: What are four attitudes that destroy harmony within a fellowship? Describe how each operates and why it hinders unity. Answers will include:

- *Selfish ambition.* This is eagerness for success that tramples over anyone who might be standing in the way of that goal. In a fellowship this is the attitude that looks at other people in terms of how they can be used.
- *Vain conceit.* This is the attitude that seeks recognition at all costs. When this attitude operates in a fellowship, people are related to in terms of the recognition they can give to one, not in terms of who they are.
- *Considering yourself better than others.* This attitude looks down on those considered inferior. In a fellowship, what you get are groups that stand over against each other instead of a unity born out of a generous acceptance of all people.
- *Failure to be concerned about the interests and needs of others.* Preoccupation with one's own needs prevents the kind of giving to others that creates warmth and community.

Ask: Give personal examples—both positive and negative—of how such attitudes affect fellowship in a church.

Ask: Why is unity vital in order for a fellowship to survive outside pressure? Answers will include:

- It is hard for one person to stand against false teaching, but a loving fellowship together can resist such alteration of the gospel.
- When there is disunity, the false teachers can pit one group against another.
- People may be tempted to resist such pressure in unchristian ways unless there is a warm, wise fellowship that will absorb the pressure and maintain a clarity about how one ought to respond as a child of God.

If it is appropriate, ask the following set of questions of the whole class. If not, ask the class to think about these questions during the week.

Ask: How well do you do when it comes to avoiding ambition, conceit, and lack of interest in others? Are you a humble person? Are you part of the answer or part of the problem when it comes to harmonious relationships? Think about a specific relationship and analyze how you view and treat that other person.

Remind

Homework
Assign the units you will cover during the next session.

Comment

Maintaining Unity
by John White

The rules for maintaining Christian fellowship are simple but tough. You will find them in several parts of the New Testament. Just now I have Philippians 2:3-4 mainly in mind.

Let nothing be done through strife or vainglory (KJV).

What motivates you in the activities of your Christian group? How much of it is either competitive or an attempt to win approval?... Strife: the word in the context implies the wish to insist on your way because you resent someone else. Your proposed action may be right in itself. But what makes you push it so hard? Does Joe get under your skin and do you sense that he will oppose it? Or do you pursue the matter because of Mary's tendency to steam roller her wishes over everyone else's?

Let nothing be done through strife. Joe's and Mary's ideas may be wrong and their spirit inappropriate. But to fight them with their own weapons is to destroy fellowship. You mustn't fight them at all. The real enemy is the Sower of Discord, and to fight him you begin by putting right your feelings of strife towards Joe and Mary. Having done so, you ask God whether you are really right as to what you thought God wanted. If you are, God may require that you stand firm in your ideas. But standing firm must never be due to your feelings toward Joe and Mary.

Stick with your point if you're sure of it but without riding it to death. If other people buy Joe's and Mary's schemes, don't sulk. God can afford to wait. Be a cheerful dissenter and someone who disagrees courteously and charitably.

Let nothing be done through strife *or*

vainglory. You must do nothing in the group with the idea of exciting admiration. Have you discovered a contribution you can make? Something you excel at? Have praises been whispered in your ear? Is there someone else who is not as competent as you? *Let nothing be done through vainglory*. It kills fellowship.

Do nothing from selfishness or conceit, but in humility count others better than yourselves (Phil. 2:3).

So there's something you're good at. Of course you recognize you have your weaknesses. In fact sometimes you feel low. But you're not the lowest man on the totem pole. Would you say you're around the halfway mark? Or higher?

In the quotation I made, Paul poses an intellectual problem. How can most of us "esteem others better than" ourselves? Can we do so and remain intellectually honest? After all, we cannot *all* be the *most* inferior. That unhappy position belongs to only one of us. The rest of us range somewhere between the best and the worst. Would it not be more honest to assess yourself realistically in terms of your place in the scale of values?

By all means be realistic; but what are you measuring when you assess your worth over against Cynthia's? Your scholastic achievement? Your athletic ability? Your clothes? Your body's appearance? Your "personality"? Your spiritual knowledge? Your enthusiasm about Christian things? Your years of experience? Some aggregate of all of these?

For which one of these can you take any personal credit? If they are God-given things, they do not make you *better* than Cynthia only *more fortunate*. They should be a cause of humble gratitude. And if you have been diligent and *can* take credit for something (or think you can), it may be worth less than you think. Human efforts rate low in the divine scale of values....

Paul's position is an existential rather than an intellectual one. In discovering the gifts and virtues of others, he has been awed and overwhelmed. He realizes that the question of who is the better man is complex. But in any case it is irrelevant to him. He is more impressed by the gifts of others than by his own.

"*Let each of you look not only to his own interests, but also to the interests of others*" (Phil. 2:4).

I am excited about my new car. When people give admiring comments after church, I am gratified. I launch into an account of how I came to make such a good buy. But I am bored when Tom interrupts to tell me that *he* got a good buy on *his* car when he bought it six months ago. Doesn't Tom realize that his car is of no interest to me? Can he be aware how dull his conversation is? I steer the talk firmly back to the marvels of my own acquistion....

I pass through deep waters emotionally. Suddenly in the midst of my trouble God breaks through. A new insight turns my darkness to day, my groaning to joy. In the fellowship meeting I share what has happened with my brothers and sisters who praise God with me for it. But Bill seizes the opportunity to tell every body about how God has met *his* need during the week. I feel it would be improper not to let him have his say, but I feel restless as the interest of the group turns from me to Bill. To cover my restlessness I join the chorus of thanksgiving for what God has done for Bill. But my heart is not in the matter. My problems and blessings seem vastly more important than Bill's. The fellowship meeting has suddenly gone flat.

Why is it so hard for me to be interested in Bill's joys and sorrows? Can it be that I am looking to my fellow Christians for something I should really look to God for? It is true that God gave me their fellowship partly for my comfort, but perhaps I am leaning on them too much. For when God is my source of joy and comfort I find I have more ability to give to the group than I have need to receive from it.

The rule must stand then: *Look not every man on his own things*. The moment I find the rule hard to carry out, I know that the dry sponge which is my heart is sucking too greedily for the love of those around me. It cannot be squeezed to give forth sweetness. It needs to be heavy with the love of God, yielding its refreshment to the slightest pressure from my fellow Christians. As I find my joys in him, so my capacity to give will exceed my need to receive.—*The Fight* (Downers Grove, Ill: InterVarsity Press, 1976), pp. 143-148.

John 1:1-2 Heb 12:2-4
" 13:13-20 Rev 5/19

UNIT 6—The Humility of Christ/Philippians 2:5-11

Ready

Now you are about to get into some *theology*. At first glance, Philippians appears to be a rather simple letter dealing with personal issues that arise out of the experience of Paul and the Philippians. But suddenly in chapter two we are confronted with the most amazing hymn in which there are the profoundest insights into the nature of God.

Now, I don't think Paul intended to make a major theological statement here. He was simply quoting this hymn as a sort of sermon illustration by way of making his point that self-sacrificing humility is the path to unity in the church. The hymn is almost an aside in the flow of the letter—probably because the Philippians were already familiar with it. Paul simply reminds them of what they already know.

But for us, coming across this hymn is like finding a diamond in the desert or a pearl in the sea. We are amazed and gladdened and astonished. And when we really hear what is being said in these verses, in wonder we suck in our breath and then breathe out a prayer of praise to God for his incredible work of love.

Think about what is asserted in the hymn. First, it states that the Creator-God and Jesus Christ are, in essence, the very same. Nearly twenty centuries later this observation is commonplace for the Christian (though no less amazing). We are familiar with the diety of Christ and the doctrine of the Trinity. But this was not so for the people to whom Paul wrote. That a man might become like a god—they had heard of this. That the gods might from time to time "visit" in human form, wearing flesh like a mask—this too the old tales spoke of. But generally these "old tales" were understood to be just that—"tales." That the real God, the High God, the God of Abraham, Isaac, and Jacob would come down into time and space and assume human form, well, this was a whole different dimension.

Furthermore, when Jesus came he was not "play-acting." He came and lived and taught and died as a real man. No mere mask for this Jesus.

How incredible. Surely this was and is the most exciting news on the whole planet. That God should visit his creation is awesome enough—but that he should do so as one of his creatures, well . . . who could have imagined it?

Who *could* have imagined it? (This is the second thing to be noted about this hymn.) This was not at all what the people of that era would have expected. According to their world view, this was not the way the gods acted. The gods stayed aloof. They remained "in charge." They kept to themselves. But this God—not only did he come but he came as a *servant*. "How can this be?" they must have asked. "The gods don't serve. It works the other way around. We serve the gods." But this is what the hymn attests. Jesus, who was in every nature God, came to earth as a slave. Coming is amazing enough. But surely he would come as king? Or at least as a member of the privileged class? But no, he came into time and space as one of the anonymous mass at the bottom of the social heap.

And then what does he do? (This is the third thing we should notice.) He allows himself to be killed. Who would have expected this of all things? The gods don't die. The gods have all the power on their side. They make others die. But the true God dies—and out of his death comes the very healing force that is able to cure the ills of the world.

Do you see how amazing this hymn is? It set on their head all of their presuppositions. They thought: the gods rule, not serve. The gods kill, not die. The gods remain aloof from their creation; they do not become a part of it. The gods act out of power, not out of weakness. But when Jesus came, he showed them that they were 180 degrees wrong about the true God.

We know all this, of course. But still, on what level of our personality do we know it? When we can burst through our assumptions and view this story with fresh eyes, then we capture again the wonder of it all. And not only this. We are changed by what we have seen.

So, this is your task today as teacher: to help your class grasp again the wonder of the incarnation.

Aim

☐ To understand the wonder of the incarnation . . . and so to be challenged anew to worship God and live in his way.

☐ To probe the descent of Jesus into time and space . . . and then to learn from his example about how we ought to live.

☐ To examine the ascent of Jesus into eternity . . . and so learn his true nature and what this means to us.

☐ To wrestle with how to capture in words the dual nature of Jesus . . . and so be exposed to various christological controversies.

Fire

Begin by saying: "Today we are going to look at the most important passage in Philippians. Now, it must be stated that the hymn in 2:6-11 is probably not the most important part of this letter from the point of view of the Philippians. They already knew this hymn. At this point in the letter it serves mainly as a illustration. Paul's purpose was not to teach them about the nature of Jesus. It was to use Christ as an

37

example of the kind of humility that he is urging on them. If they can become like this, then the sort of unity will emerge that will enable them to resist the pressure being leveled against them.

"For us however, coming across this early hymn is exhilarating as we grasp again the wonder of the incarnation. Or, at least, it ought to be exhilarating. It may not be for the simple reason that we have heard this story over and over again. We live in a culture that reflects this story in its art, literature, history, and social consciousness. Our familiarity with it has muted its impact on us.

"So, what we want to do today is to open ourselves to this passage in such a way that we grasp again the wonder of it all. Let's pray and ask God to give us this kind of vision:
'Lord, God, what you have done for us in time and space is beyond imagination. Who could have thought that you would work this way? Who could have imagined that you loved us so much that you would actually come to our planet and then die for our salvation? Open our eyes to see all this again with a fresh sense of wonder. We pray in Jesus' name. Amen.' "

Discuss

Christ Descending
Read to the class Philippians 2:6-11.

Mini-Lecture: Use the material in the **Ready** section to structure a brief lecture that will help the class see what this passage is saying.

Ask: What strikes you about this passage? Use the responses of the class to extend the discussion of what God did in Christ Jesus.

Read aloud the passage by C. S. Lewis "Christ Descending to Ascend" found in the **Comment** section. [You might want to practice reading this to yourself before the class.]

Discuss the personal implications of what Jesus did. Begin by stating: "Jesus provides for us a model of radical humility. His example of how we ought to relate to one another runs counter to our cultural norms. We are not big on humility, preferring instead power and domination." Then . . .

Ask: What does this example on the part of Jesus say to our culture about how we are meant to relate to others? Answers will include:

☐ We are meant to relate out of humility, not self-centeredness.

☐ We are to serve, not dominate.

☐ True power comes via weakness.

Ask: Reflect on how well you did during the past week in your personal relationships concerning humility. Would anyone like to share what they discovered—

Christ Ascending
Begin by saying: "The self-humiliation of Jesus is not the whole story. Part two in this divine drama involves the lifting up of Christ by God."

Ask: According to this hymn, who is Jesus? How can we define his nature? Answers will include:

☐ He is God.

☐ He is the King of the universe.

☐ He is the servant/savior who died for his people.

☐ He is Lord.

☐ He is that Power before whom all other powers bow.

Ask: In contrast, who do people in general view Jesus to be? What titles do they use for him by which to define how they understand his nature? Answers will include:

☐ A religious prophet.

☐ A great teacher.

☐ A religious fanatic.

☐ A myth (he never existed).

☐ A social reformer.

☐ A good man who got caught up in affairs beyond his control.

☐ A mystic.

☐ A magician.

Ask: How did you come to discover the true nature of Jesus? What difference has this discovery made in who you are and how you live?

Christ Defined
End this session with the following mini-lecture: "It really is not easy to define in words the true nature of Jesus Christ. Once you get beyond the assertion that he is fully divine and fully human, the going gets tough. The more you try to state exactly what this means, the more the words seem to fail you. The history of the church provides ample evidence of how difficult it is to capture within a verbal formulation the full nature of Jesus. Especially in the early years there was a whole series of controversies as the church struggled to express its views on Jesus over against various heresies that emerged.

"One set of heresies affirmed the humanity of Jesus but failed to do justice to his deity.

These include:

- The Ebionites and Cerinthians who taught that Jesus was the son of Mary and Joseph. They said that it was at his baptism that he was united with the eternal Christ and became the Son of God.

- The Adoptianists and Dynamic Monarchians who taught that Jesus was the adoptive Son of God. They said that the divine Spirit descended upon Jesus—who was merely a man although perfect and born of a virgin—at the time of his baptism.

- The Nestorians who split Jesus Christ into two distinct persons, one human and one divine, rather than seeing a real union of the two natures in the one person.

"Other heresies affirmed the godhood of Jesus but failed to do justice to his humanity. These include:

- The Docetists who taught that Jesus was not a real man. He only appeared to be one.

- The Modalistic Monarchians who taught that Jesus was the incarnation of God the Father.

- The Apollinarians who taught that Christ had really only a divine nature.

- The Eutychians who taught that Jesus' human nature was swallowed up by his divine nature.

"Don't worry too much if all this seems strange and bizarre. These ideas reflect more than anything else the struggles of the early church to come to grips with how to express in words who Jesus truly was so as to do justice to his dual nature. These are not live issues for the church today—with the possible exception of docetism.

"However, there is one theory concerning the nature of Jesus that is closer to our own times and is still being discussed. This is the so-called Kenotic question which probes the meaning of Christ's self-emptying. This issue is raised, of course, by the text we have been studying—Philippians 2:5-11. The word 'kenotic' is derived from the Greek word used in 2:7 and translated 'he emptied himself.' The essence of this theory is stated by M. M. Creed; 'The Divine Logos by His Incarnation divested Himself of His divine attributes of omniscience and omnipotence, so that in His incarnate life the Divine Person is revealed and solely revealed through a human consciousness. Many scholars would take exception to this idea saying that it was not his deity he laid aside but his glory and his high position. Once again, we see the difficulty of defining exactly the nature of Jesus.

"If you are interested in all this—it is called Christology—you might want to consult a church history textbook where you can read in great detail about the early christological controversies. Or you might prefer browsing through a basic systematic theology textbook to see how theologians wrestle with the same issues. In any case, the important thing is for us to affirm the full deity and the full humanity of Jesus—even while we struggle to understand fully what those statements mean."[1]

Remind

Homework: This week, ponder the mystery of the incarnation. See what else you can discover about the coming of Jesus.

---

[1]These comments are drawn in large part from various entries in *The New International Dictionary of the Christian Church*, ed. J. D. Douglas (Grand Rapids, MI: Zondervan Publishing House), 1978.

Comment

Christ Descending to Ascend

by C. S. Lewis

In the Christian story God descends to re-ascend. He comes down; down from the heights of absolute being into time and space, down into humanity; down further still, if embryologists are right, to recapitulate in the womb ancient and pre-human phases of life; down to the very roots and seabed of the Nature He has created. But He goes down to come up again and bring the whole ruined world up with Him. One has the picture of a strong man stooping lower and lower to get himself underneath some great complicated burden. He must stoop in order to lift, he must almost disappear under the load before he incredibly straightens his back and marches off with the whole mass swaying on his shoulders. Or one may think of a diver, first reducing himself to nakedness, then glancing in mid-air, then gone with a splash, vanished, rushing down through green and warm water into black and cold water, down through increasing pressure into the death-like region of ooze and slime and old decay; then up again, back to colour and light, his lungs almost bursting, till suddenly he breaks surface again, holding in his hand the dripping, precious thing that he went down to recover. He and it are both coloured now that they have come up into the light: down below, where it lay colourless in the dark, he lost his colour too.—*Miracles* (London: Collins/Fontana Books, 1960) pp. 115-116.

UNIT 7—Shining as Stars/Philippians 2:12-18

Ready

"Shine like stars." What a beautiful image! It is by means of this image that Paul sums up what will happen if the Philippians follow his instructions. They will "shine like stars" in the midst of a generation that is "crooked and depraved."

This "shining," however, is dependent upon their capacity to deal with disunity. When they develop the ability to live together in unity as a loving community of God's people, then they will indeed shine. The resultant unity will be so different and so appealing that they as a community will be noticed—because the brightest point always stands out. In this way the gospel will be promoted—because people will want to know the source of this remarkable togetherness. This is the reason for all Paul's instructions: when they "cure" the ailment of disunity, the gospel will be advanced.

It is my sense that we who are a part of the contemporary American church need to listen with great care to what Paul has to say about disunity. We certainly have our share of it. The problem is not that there are a lot of different churches or that there are hundreds of denominations. The problem is that these churches and denominations do not get along very well with each other. Disunity has become a fact of life for us which we are all too content to accept.

Think about it. Disunity is all around us. We often don't get along very well with the other churches in our own community. We certainly don't have much that is good to say about other denominations. We even have problems getting along with everybody in our own church. No wonder we don't "shine like stars" to anybody!

I have often wondered: what if we all listened to Paul? Can you imagine the impact in America if the churches healed their disunity? Talk about shining like beacons in a place of darkness and confusion!

I suppose all this is dreaming. Healing the disunity in the churches of a nation seems an impossible vision. Still, we could do it because what Paul says here is absolutely true. If we renounce self-interest in its various forms and embrace the kind of humility that reaches out to others, unity would flow automatically.

But even if we can't solve the problem of disunity in the churches of America (and certainly our own fallen nature and the fallen nature of our world would make this ultimately impossible), there is one level on which we can all practice what Paul preaches. We can strive for unity in our own lives. We can aim at unity in the church we attend. This will involve correcting our own part in the disunity that exists there. We can also deal with disunity when it strikes in our businesses, in our communities, in our nation, even in our own homes. It seems to me that what Paul says here by way of curing disunity in the church is just as applicable to these other situations. Think about what could happen if we each would begin to deal with disunity in the small spheres we occupy. Unity would start to spread. And as it spreads, who knows how wide it will reach? Dreams again, but still. . . .

In any case, here is how this teaching unit is structured. First, you will look at the text in order to discern once again those attitudes and actions that bring about unity in contrast to those that bring about disunity. Then, you will have a chance to see how these insights apply in three specific situations—your church, your home, and your personal life.

You should be warned that this may not be the easiest of discussions. In order to move from disunity to unity we are called upon to do what the Philippians had to do. First, we have to admit that there is a problem. Then, we have to "own" that problem by identifying in our own lives the personal attitudes that bring about disunity. (And who likes to admit such a thing?) Finally, we have to renounce these negative attitudes by embracing the opposite, unity-producing attitudes. It is not easy to bring about change at this level. It is not easy to face those things in ourselves that create disunity.

If your class is sufficiently open and honest, this can be a discussion with great potential. If not (and the fact is, not all groups develop the kind of intimacy required by such a discussion) then you may have to keep the conversation on a more general, non-personal level. In this latter case, pray that people will hear and apply these key principles on their own. In both cases, of course, the best place to try out these ideas is in the context of the class itself.

Aim

☐ To note the process by which unity comes about . . . and so grasp how disunity is cured via the dynamic of insight, renunciation, and embracing the good.

☐ To understand what Paul means when he says that we must work at salvation while at the same time God does the work . . . and so discover the balance necessary in the Christian life.

☐ To note those attitudes that bring unity or disunity . . . and apply these insights to our core relationships.

Fire

Begin this session by saying: "Today we are going to do two things. First, we will try to understand what Paul means when he says that we are 'to work out (our) salvation with fear and trembling, for it is God who works in you to will and to act.' This is a key principle of the Christian life. If we grasp what Paul is saying in these two verses, then we will have understood on a fundamental level what it means to be a Christian. Then second, we will apply this general principle in a very specific way. We will ask: 'What does it mean to grow in unity in those relationships that form the core of our lives?' The particular topic by which we will test out this general principle has not, of course, been chosen at random. Unity is the issue that Paul has been dealing with ever since 1:27."

Discuss

Working Out Our Salvation

Ask: What does Paul mean when he says that *we* are to work out our own salvation but it is *God* who works in us? Proceed to answer this question yourself by way of a mini-lecture in which you make the following points:

☐ There are two sides to the Christian life: what we do and what God does.

☐ By implication, if we neglect one side, our life gets out of balance.

☐ The person who sits back and quietly, piously, and genuinely seeks to "let God do it all in my life" is refusing a God-given responsibility to act in ways pleasing to God. Such a *passive view of Christianity* can result in a lifestyle in which a person both refuses to take responsibility for what he or she does or does not do, and refuses to use fully the gifts God has given for ministry.

☐ The person who is an aggressive go-getter for God, full of kingdom building plans often takes on too much responsibility and so is easily discouraged when things do not go well or when others fail to jump behind all his or her great ideas. Such an *activist view of Christianity* can result in a compulsive lifestyle in which a person never listens—to others or to God, with the result that they burn out or get bitter.

☐ A balanced Christian life is one in which God and his will is actively sought in the silence while simultaneously that person works at being what God wants in all spheres of life.

☐ This is to recognize that living the life of a Christian takes determined effort and on-going activity on our part.

☐ This is to recognize that we cannot generate either our own desire to live for God much less the energy to do so. We need consciously to open ourselves to what God is doing in and around us.

Ask: Which side of this tension do you tend to live on? As a Christian, are you more an activist who is busy in God's work or a pacifist who waits on God? How can you achieve more balance in your life?

Read, by way of concluding this topic, the article by John White entitled "God's Work or Yours?" found in the **Comment** section.

Unity as a Way of Life

Introduce this section by giving the following mini-lecture. The material in the **Ready** section will be of use to you. Point out that:

☐ Unity does not just happen. You have to work at producing it.

☐ The dynamic by which one moves from disunity to unity is three-fold. [Put each italicized point on the chalk board as you mention it.] It begins with *insight:* you must identify in yourself those attitudes that produce disunity. It moves to *renunciation:* you must reject these negative attitudes. It ends with *embracing the new:* you open yourself to those attitudes which bring unity.

☐ Producing unity requires both our activity and God's intervention. We must identify negative attitudes and embrace positive ones at the same time that God brings insight and provides motivation to act on what we see.

☐ What then are the attitudes that produce unity and what are those that produce disunity? Let's begin by scanning this whole section from 1:27 to 2:18 in order to identify the two sets of attitudes. Then we will discuss how each does its work.

Ask: What attitudes and actions produce disunity and why? [List each category on the chalk board or overhead projector.] Answers include:

☐ *Selfish ambition* (2:3). This kind of preoccupation with one's own career and success makes it difficult to cooperate wholeheartedly with others.

☐ *Vain conceit* (2:3). When recognition is your motive, then it is hard for you to generate any enthusiasm for the kind of ministry in which you might not get credit for what is accomplished.

☐ *Self interest* (2:4). When you cannot look outside your own needs and interests to those of others, it is difficult to feel much of a bond to others much less be willing to aid them enthusiastically.

☐ *Complaining* (2:14). When your attitude to others (especially to those who are the leaders) is that of complaining about what they do or do not do, you cannot join them with much enthusiasm in a common project.

☐ *Arguing* (2:14). When your posture toward others is disputive, then you tend to push them away rather than draw them to you.

Ask: What attitudes and actions produce unity and why? (Make a list.) Answers will include:

☐ *Humility* (2:3). Others are drawn to the genuinely humble person.

☐ *Be oriented to the interests of others* (2:4). When people give themselves to the needs and interests of others, others are drawn to them.

☐ *Servanthood* (2:7). Service given to others begets, in response, service by them and thus people are drawn together.

☐ *Blamelessness* (2:15). In contrast to complaining and arguing, strive to live in such a way that no one can fault your behavior. In this way no exterior barrier is raised that pushes people away.

☐ *Purity* (2:15). The truly good person who is genuinely pure (as far as that is possible in a fallen world with a fallen nature) can risk transparency. Such openness, in turn, produces deep relationships.

☐ *Faultlessness* (2:15). When a person strives to be the kind of person God wants, this creates unity between people of like mind.

In this next section of the discussion, take these general principles and apply them to three situations: the church, the home, and personal relationships in general. Whether you ask the second question (which involves personal sharing) or use only the general statement will depend upon your group.

Ask: Think about *churches* you have known. How do each of the attitudes above promote or destroy unity in a church? Be as specific as possible. Which of these attitudes characterize our church at the moment?

Ask: Think about *homes* you have been in. How do each of the above attitudes promote or destroy unity in a home? Be as specific as possible. Which of these attitudes characterize your own home?

Ask: Think about *relationships* in general. How do each of the above attitudes promote or destroy unity in a relationship? Be as specific as possible. Which of these attitudes characterize your own relationships?

Ask: If the Christian life involves a balance between our actions and God's actions, what is required of *us* when it comes to promoting unity? What is *God's* part? How do the two fit together?

Remind

Homework

Comment

God's Work or Yours?

by John White

"Let go and let God." This was a catch-phrase of obscure origins from the late nineteenth century. A college student is alleged to have written on six postcards the letters L E T G O D and placed the six cards on the mantleplace of his room. As a draught blew down the letter "D," he is said to have discovered the secret of *letting God* control his life by *letting go* of it himself.

Many people have found the words helpful. Nevertheless, they raise a serious issue about holiness over which Christians disagree. Some see holiness as a work of God to which the Christian makes no contribution. My part as a Christian is simply to relinquish control. His part is to work through me. My efforts to strive after holiness will be unavailing. In me, that is in my flesh, dwells no good thing so that I have nothing of value to contribute. I therefore trust, that is, I *rest* in his goodness. I do not struggle to control my temper but allow Christ to handle my angry feelings. I say with Paul, "Not I but Christ." It is as though, like a sea captain, I have been up to this point at the helm of my life, and now Another is going to take over. Even faith is seen as a passivity of the will, a resting and a relaxing, not a seizing or appropriating.

I want to call this view the *passive* view of holiness in contrast with what might be called the *active* view by which the Christian is called on to "wrestle and fight and pray."

Teachers of the active schools stress what they call "the means of grace." Yielding may be good but must not exclude watching and prayer, meditation on the Scriptures, fellowship with other believers, a careful effort to "maintain good works," a deliberate attempt to refrain from sin and to perform active Christian duties.

You will be puzzled as you talk to exponents of both schools to find they can give convincing and sincere testimonies to the blessings they have received as a result of practicing what seem to be conflicting principles. All schools are agreed that *faith is the key issue*. All schools are agreed that human efforts alone are unavailing and that the power for holy living must come from God. All schools are agreed that the basis of sanctification is God's intervention in the incarnation, death, resurrection and ascension of his Son, Jesus Christ, and that the help is *mediated by the Holy Spirit who brings about the believer's union with Christ*. But given the general points of agreement the words and phrases used become confusing and contradictory.

It need not surprise us that there should be

confusion and difficulty. In the first place the New Testament itself seems to express both points of view. "Work out your own salvation with fear and trembling," writes Paul to the Philippians, apparently espousing an *active* view of the Christian life. Yet with no pause he goes on, "for [because] God is at work in you, both to will and to work for his good pleasure" (Phil. 2:12-13). Now if you had only the words in the second part of the sentence, you might conclude that a Christian should lie passive in the hands of a God who actively worked within him. And notice. God not only makes a man do what God wants. God actually makes the decision inside him, that is, causes him to *will*.

Yet to Paul there seems to be no conflict between the first part of the sentence and the second. We are to work because God is working in us. The New Testament consistently presents both what I have called the passive and the active approaches to holiness without any sense of contradiction.

One of the key expressions of the passive teaching of sanctification is "yield." Now in only one place in the New Testament are we urged to yield to God. In Romans 6:13-19 the expression occurs several times over. But scholars assure me that even here the word does not mean a passive lying in God's hands so much as a presenting of ourselves to be of service to God.

Is there anything passive about Paul's instruction toward the end of Romans?

> Let love be genuine; hate what is evil, hold fast to what is good; love one another with brotherly affection; outdo one another in showing honor. Never flag in zeal, be aglow with the Spirit, serve the Lord. Rejoice in your hope, be patient in tribulation, be constant in prayer. Contribute to the needs of the saints, practice hospitality. (Rom. 12:9-13)

Of course, none of us could obey these instructions apart from the power of the Holy Spirit. But *yielding to the Spirit consists of obeying the Spirit's directions, by faith and in the Spirit's power.*

How do we acquire the attributes of a holy character? By waiting? Or by working? Notice the curious paradox at the beginning of Peter's second epistle. He begins by telling us that God has "granted to us his precious and very great promises, that through these you may escape from the corruption that is in the world because of passion, and become partakers of the divine nature" (2 Pet. 1:4). It is all of God. And God has given us his all.

So what are we to do? Do we rest in the promises and yield to the divine nature within? What Peter actually says is,

> *For this very reason make every effort* to supplement your faith with virtue, and virtue with knowledge, and knowledge with self-control, and self-control with steadfastness, and steadfastness with godliness, and godliness with brotherly affection, and brotherly affection with love. (2 Pet. 1:5-7)

Use all the power at your disposal to put God's gifts to good use!

Let there be no misunderstanding. Without God's Spirit within, our efforts are futile. No good thing could spring from our corrupt and sinful hearts. But we have been redeemed and we have been sanctified. We have been set apart for God's use. Let us then agree with God in the matter. If yielding means bowing down to him as King, let us day by day, hour by hour yield every part of our beings in allegiance to him. Let us reserve no part of our lives to serve selfish interests and ambitions. But having done that, let us assume the whole armor of God and by miraculous strength declare war on all that is evil within and without.

Stand then in His great might,
   With all his strength endued
And take, to arm you for the fight,
   The panoply of God.

— *The Fight* (Downers Grove, Ill.: InterVarsity Press, 1976), excerpts taken from pp. 190-194.

UNIT 8—Timothy and Epaphroditus/Philippians 2:19-30

Ready

In the past few units, Paul has been dealing with the issue of disunity and how to cure it. Up to this point, he has been addressing this problem on a somewhat theoretical level. He has pointed out why the Philippians need to be united (so that they can stand against the outside forces pressing in on them as a church). He has identified those attitudes that create disunity (vain conceit, self interest, complaining, and arguing). He has likewise noted those attitudes which bring unity (humility, interest in the interests of others, servanthood, and a life that is blameless, pure, and faultless). But so far all this has been cast in general terms.

However, here in this unit and in the following three units, this generality gives way to specifics. First, Paul talks about his relationship with two of his colleagues, Timothy and Epaphroditus. This becomes an example of the kind of unity that he has been urging on the Philippians. Next (in Units 9 and 10) Paul looks at the opposite kind of relationship. How do you deal with your enemies? What about those people who seek to destroy the Christian faith? If unity is what you strive for with your friends, family, and colleagues, what is your posture toward those who would undermine the faith? Thus he discusses the false teachers who are at work in Philippi. Finally, in contrast to the positive example of good relationships between Christians with which he began, in Unit 11 Paul turns his attention to a negative example. There he discusses the troubling relationship between two of the leaders in the Philippian church.

As a result Paul's letter becomes a *case study in relationships*. Today you will be examining the positive example—Paul's relationship with Timothy and Epaphroditus. What he has to say here about relationships is, however, indirect. It comes in the context of "news." Ostensibly, Paul is reporting on these two men—giving their friends information both about their well-being and about their plans. But in doing this, he is also saying to the Philippians: "This is how we are meant to relate to one another."

Of course, this is the sign of a good teacher. Paul first presented the "theory" on how to create unity (1:27-2:18). Then he fleshes out these concepts by means of examples. Your aim today as teacher is to get at what Paul says here about good relationships.

Aim

☐ To examine Paul's relationship with Timothy and Epaphroditus . . . and so to note the characteristics of a relationship between Christians in which there is unity.

☐ To note how the relationship between these men models what Paul says about the attitudes that produce unity . . . and thus to understand better Paul's statement in 2:3-4.

☐ To apply these principles to the relationships of those in the class . . . and thus grasp the strengths and weaknesses of our relationships.

Fire

Begin this session by saying: "Today we start on a new section in Philippians. From 2:19 to 4:9 there are three sets of case studies by which Paul illustrates his words about unity. By discussing the characteristics of unity and disunity he gives us a powerful glimpse into the meaning of friendship, the nature of koinonia, and the process of discipleship. First, in 2:19-30, Paul touches on his own relationship to two of his colleagues—Timothy and Epaphroditus. This is the unit we will study today. This is an example of how Christians ought to relate to one another. Then in 3:1-4:1 Paul looks at the relationship between the Philippians and those enemies of the gospel that have been seeking to disrupt their church. This is an example of how to deal with those from without who would destroy our unity. Finally, in 4:2-9 Paul examines a troubling relationship between two of the leaders in the Philippian church. This is an example of how unity can be destroyed from within.

"In other words, what Paul does in this next to the last section of his letter is to flesh out his teaching about unity in relationships. Notice how Paul has structured the letter to the Philippians. He begins by giving us the theory. In 1:27-2:18 he told us *how to develop relationships* in which there is a sense of unity. Then here in 2:19 to 4:9, he looks at *the actual experience of being in relationship*. He does this first by means of a *positive example*—his relationship with his two colleagues. In contrast he offers a *negative example* which they all know about: the dispute between Euodia and Syntyche. Finally, in opposition to the positive and the negative example of relationships between Christians, Paul looks at the relationship between the church and those who are its enemies.

"Do you see how Philippians is unfolding? Paul begins by talking about the advance of the gospel and how this is the key thing for which he is willing to pay whatever price is demanded (1:12-26). Then he turns from *his* situation to *their* situation and urges them to develop the same attitude. They must work to advance the gospel. But, he points out, this is made difficult because of the false teachers who would pervert the gospel. In order to stand against them, however, the Philippians must be unified *v. 19 — What is Trust?*

as a church. It is this necessity that launches Paul's call to unity and his instructions about how to achieve it (1:27-2:18). Now in this new section he fleshes out his theoretical words about unity by offering the three case studies of relationships.

"We need to look carefully at what Paul says here in this first example. This is the positive example. This is how it ought to be. His relationship with Timothy and with Epaphroditus serves as an illustration of how Christians ought to stand together in love and unity. We can learn much from a careful examination of this material."

Discuss

Timothy
Ask: In this passage, what do we learn about Timothy and about Paul's relationship to him? Answers will include:

- Paul has the kind of relationship with Timothy that allows him to "send" Timothy on a trip to Philippi (vv. 19, 23).
- Paul has a unique relationship with Timothy: "I have no one else like him" (v. 20).
- Timothy is a special friend and colleague to Paul (v. 20).
- Like Paul, Timothy's ministry is genuine. He really cares for people (v. 20).
- The prime motivating force for Timothy is the promotion of the interests of Jesus Christ (v. 21).
- Timothy has a proven ministry (v. 22).
- Timothy is like a son to Paul (v. 22).
- Their relationship is in the context of ministry (v. 22).

Epaphroditus
Ask: In this passage, what do we learn about Epaphroditus and about Paul's relationship to him? Answers will include:

- Paul identifies five roles which Epaphroditus played: (1) he was a believer, a Christian brother; (2) he was also a co-worker in the gospel; (3) a fellow soldier in the fight against the enemies of the gospel; (4) a chosen messenger sent by the Philippians; and (5) one who ministered to Paul's needs.
- Each of these roles is positive and mention of them is affirming to Epaphroditus.
- Each of these roles involves serving others.
- In this instance, Paul is on the receiving end of Epaphroditus' ministry.
- Epaphroditus' illness prevented the completion of his task, but now Paul has a new role for him—to carry his letter to Philippi and to be his emissary there to help deal with the problems the Philippians face.
- Epaphroditus risked everything—even his very life—to serve the gospel.

Colleagues and Co-workers
Give the following mini-lecture by way of reflection on the nature of relationships between Christians. Begin by saying: "What are the characteristics of the relationship between Paul and these two men that have created such unity? Notice the following:

- Their shared ministry focuses on the needs of others. They are united in caring for others and for each other. When we serve others, we develop a deep bond with those who participate in that caring process. In other words, unity often arises out of mission.
- There is a common respect for the ability, commitment, and roles played by each person. Paul valued deeply Timothy's track record in dealing with difficulties. He is fully confident in Timothy's ability to carry on his own ministry when he is unable to do so himself. Paul values deeply the self-sacrifice of Epaphroditus on his behalf. Confidence in the gifts and abilities of others generates a sense of unity.
- There is warmth and love toward one another. Theirs is not merely a 'professional' relationship. They love each other and are eager to give to each other and depend on each other. Trust for others, developed in the context of mutual love, is key to unity in relationships.
- Their relationship to one another is expressed in terms of 'family,' with words like 'son,' 'brother,' and 'father' being used. Deep relationships emerge when we treat others not merely as colleagues but as 'kin.'
- Together they exemplify what Paul said in 2:3-4 about the attitudes that produce unity. They are not motivated by 'selfish ambition,' nor are they driven by 'vain conceit.' Instead, they really do look out for the interests of others. These same attitudes generate unity in our relationships."

Ask: Think about the relationships within your own church. How do they match up to this model?

Ask: Think about your relationships with others—colleagues, co-workers, family, friends. How do they match up to this model?

Remind

Homework

UNIT 9—No Confidence in the Flesh/Philippians 3:1-11

Ready

It seems strange that in the midst of a long and impassioned plea for unity Paul stops, seemingly in midstream, in order to castigate a group of Jewish missionaries. On one level, of course, this is understandable. These missionaries are the reason for his call to unity. The Philippian church will not be able to resist the allure of their message if there is internal fragmentation and fighting. But, on another level we ask: shouldn't this unity which Paul is urging extend beyond the bounds of the church? Why not strive for unity with these teachers instead of opposing them?

I think the answer is clear. These are not merely a group of neutral religionists who happen to have a different perspective than Paul. In point of fact, they are in active opposition to the church. They would like to see it changed into something quite different. As a result, they must be resisted if the church is to survive.

Furthermore, they are not merely attacking Christianity. They are actively seeking to win converts from it. They are missionaries. Their aim is to convert Christians to Judaism. In this regard, they are particularly dangerous because what they preach is near enough to the gospel to appear authentic. After all, the God they worship is the God and Father of the Lord Jesus Christ. He is the God who is worshiped and honored by Christians. What they are saying is: "You want to please God? Great. So do we. Now here is how to do it. Keep the law, get circumcised and then God will be pleased." At first glance what they are saying does not appear to be so awful. "Obey the rules." After all, they are God's rules. The problem is, as Paul points out, once you introduce the idea that you can, by your own effort, earn salvation, then you undercut grace and mute the meaning of the Cross.

There is another aspect to all this. Apparently, these Jewish teachers are also appealing to some of the pre-Christian religious sentiments of the Philippians. In the next unit of this letter it becomes apparent that part of the appeal of their message is due to its promise of perfection. They are saying that if you just keep all the rules, especially certain ritual observances, you will be "perfect." The promise of perfection was characteristic of many cults that existed in the first century.

So these missionaries must be resisted—for three reasons. One, because they actively oppose the church. They are not a neutral force. Two, because their gospel undercuts the very foundation of the Christian faith. You can't have grace if you promote works as the key to the religious life. Works negates grace. Three, because they arouse in people latent religious aspirations for perfection when in fact, as Paul will show in the next unit, the Christian walk is one of ongoing striving, not one of having arrived at a state of perfection.

So back to the question of unity in relationships. It is clear that these folks must be opposed. But should all those who stand outside the church be considered enemies? This is where the danger lies. At times, as Christians, we are all too quick to see enemies everywhere. We label all those who are not one with us as being against us (even those in other Christian denominations). This is clearly not what Paul is urging. In fact he never says "Actively oppose these missionaries." He simply says, "Watch out for them. Don't get taken in by their message." This is quite a different thing than devoting oneself to defining and destroying enemies.

In today's lesson you will be touching on this question of "enemies," but your focus will be on the issue of accomplishment and what it means to live a life that is genuinely Christian. The religious Jews of the first century made a big deal out of what they did for God. Personal accomplishment was what got them into heaven. We rightly disapprove of that kind of self-righteousness, and yet, at times it looks awfully much like we too are trying to be big deals in the kingdom of God. In contrast, Paul (who was a certifiable "big deal") saw all that he did as of no value. Only one thing mattered: knowing Christ. What does his single-minded passion for Jesus have to teach us as we struggle to live for Christ in the twentieth century?

Aim

☐ To note Paul's accomplishments and how he viewed them . . . and then wrestle with how we view our accomplishments.

☐ To examine Paul's passion for knowing Jesus . . . and then wrestle with what it means to live out Christ's death and resurrection.

☐ To note specifically who Paul is opposing and what he urges . . . so as not to think that all who are not Christians must be resisted.

Fire

Begin this session by saying: "We get quite a remarkable glimpse into Paul in this unit. In the process of listing his accomplishments so he can point out that they mean nothing, we come to realize that prior to his conversion to Christ he was an authentically 'big deal' in Judaism. He was the elite of the elite. He had it all going for him—lineage, achievement, religious zeal. In terms of first-century standards, you name it, Paul had done it.

Concision - Those in the Apostles time who put to much importance on circumcision

"But he turned his back on all that. From the standpoint of his Jewish compatriots he gave up all his education, all his accomplishments. He turned his back on his culture and his people. He forsook his allegiance to the elite religious organization he was part of. And for what? To join an obscure sect which followed the teachings of a dead leader who had been condemned as a criminal. It just didn't make sense.

"In this passage, Paul shows how it does make sense. And in so doing he causes us to question (1) how we relate to our religious accomplishments and (2) where our real religious aspirations actually lie. Let's look at both issues through the grid of Paul's life. We'll examine what Paul did and was as we wrestle with the question of accomplishments. And then we will look at what he became and why as we wrestle with the question of what lies at the heart of the Christian message."

Discuss

On Being a Big Deal for God

Ask: On what did Paul base the assertion that if anyone could trust in accomplishments, he could? Answers will include:

- He was circumcised from birth, i.e., he was always a Jew.
- He was of the people of Israel, i.e., he was a member of the chosen people of God.
- He was from the tribe of Benjamin, i.e., the elite tribe that had always remained faithful to God.
- He was a Hebrew of the Hebrews, i.e., although born in a Gentile region he had remained fully Jewish in culture.
- He was a Pharisee, i.e., a member of the spiritual elite in Israel.
- He was zealous to an extreme, i.e., he displayed a virtue that was highly regarded within Judaism.
- He was faultless when it came to the law, i.e., he kept the whole law despite its many and rigorous demands.

Ask: What are the kind of things Christians do that are regarded as noteworthy and of great religious value? Answers will include:

- Live a rigorous, ascetic lifestyle in which there is great sacrifice and hardship.
- Become a missionary to a needy people living in a remote land.
- Shun "worldly pleasures" such as dancing, drinking, smoking, going to the movies, etc.
- Get involved in the "right" political issues.
- Memorize a lot of the Bible and/or be an expert in theology.
- Be a leader in a big, prosperous church.
- Display the fruits of the Spirit.
- Have a national ministry.

Make the following comments: "Several things become obvious once we ask a question like this. (1) There is no single norm within Christianity for what is to be valued or prized in the religious life. Different churches will have different standards for what a highly successful Christian life looks like. (2) What is valued in one setting might not be valued in a different setting. (3) Some of what is valued is certainly good and desirable by any standard. Other activities seem to be more cultural than biblical. Still others are really anti-biblical.

"The issue, when you get down to it, is not so much what we do but how we view what we do. It becomes a question of pride. Do we do what we do as a simple reflex? The love of Christ constrains us to work in this way. Or, is it a matter of one-upmanship, of trying to be better than others, of wanting to be recognized, of trying to buy God's favor? The Pharisee fallacy was that you could buy your way into God's good graces by being good, which meant keeping the law. The problem was, when you were honest you knew you could never be good enough. In our culture today, the issue is more likely to be that we find our sense of personal worth and value by being better than others. Accomplishment is a big deal in America and we in the church are not immune from its allure.

"Actually, Jesus is the one who gave the best definition of who are the big deals in his kingdom. They are the people who serve others. The ones who are last are the ones who will be first at the great day when his kingdom dawns in all its glory."

On Being in Jesus Christ

Begin this section with these comments: "Paul is not preoccupied with his past accomplishments. He is preoccupied with Jesus Christ. What is really on his heart is the surpassing worth of knowing Christ. This is not a new theme in this letter, of course. It pervades every point Paul makes. But here it comes out clearly. This is what Christians are to give themselves over to: knowing Jesus Christ fully. (He will develop this idea more fully in the next unit.) Their purpose in life is to know Christ, period. Let's examine what he says here about Jesus Christ."

Ask: What does Paul say about knowing Christ? Answers will include:

- Knowing Jesus Christ is the supreme value in life ("surpassing greatness").

- All the accomplishments of Paul prior to his conversion, though genuine, were of no value because they did not promote the end of knowing Christ.
- Paul was willing to lose all things to know Christ. He felt it was more than worth it.
- Paul's specific goal was to be found in Christ with a righteousness that comes by faith.
- Faith, not effort, is the key to knowing Christ.
- To know Christ is to be caught up in both his death and his resurrection.

Read the selection in the **Comment** section entitled: "Living Christ's Redemption and Resurrection." Introduce it by saying: "Verse 10 rings of mystery and depth: 'I want to know Christ and the power of his resurrection and the fellowship of sharing in his sufferings, becoming like him in his death.' This is not a concept that we are going to get hold of easily or quickly. What does it mean to live out the suffering and resurrection of Christ? Listen to Father Michel Quoist—author of the widely read *Prayers of Life*—as he wrestles with these concepts."

On Dealing with Enemies

Begin this section by saying: "There is one more theme that we need to touch on. What about those Jewish missionaries that are creating such stress in the Philippian church? How are the Philippians to deal with them? How are we to deal with enemies of the gospel?

"It is one thing to discuss how Christians should relate to one another. Paul has made it quite clear that such relationships ought to be characterized by love and unity. But it is another thing to discuss how to relate to those who are not brothers and sisters in the faith. Here is where we must tread very carefully. The error we might be tempted to make is to lump together all those who are not Christians and call them 'enemies' and then actively oppose them. This is *not* what Paul is calling for here. Elsewhere in his writings he tells us, 'Bless those who persecute you; bless and do not curse . . . Do not repay evil for evil . . . If it is possible, as far as it depends on you, live at peace with everyone' (Romans 12:14, 15, 18). What he does urge here in Philippians is *caution* toward a very specific group of people, *not overt hostility*. Let's examine carefully this passage in order to discover just who it is that Paul considers an enemy of the gospel and what he says about relating to them."

Ask: What are the characteristics of those whom Paul is opposing? Answers will include:

- They are those who pervert the gospel.
- They rely on their own acts of righteousness to get them into heaven, especially certain ritual observations such as circumcision.
- They are (apparently) zealously seeking converts from among the Christian church.

Ask: What specifically does Paul urge in regard to these teachers?

- Three times he urges the Philippians to "watch out" for these folks.
- The only thing that he asks the Philippians to do is to pay close attention to these false teachers so as not to be deluded into following the dead-ended path they are promoting.

At this point, if you have time, summarize your discussion by presenting the material in the **Ready** section.

Ask: What are some of the wrong ways in which we treat those we perceive to be our enemies, ways not suggested by Paul? Answers will include:

- We attempt to crush our enemies through litigation, via public pressure, by means of physical violence, etc.
- We become preoccupied with our enemies and spend our energies opposing them rather than getting on with the task of promoting the gospel.
- We are overwhelmed by them and capitulate to what they demand.

Comment

Living Christ's Redemption and Resurrection
by Michel Quoist

Man must not only receive and accept salvation from the hands of Christ; he must also participate. Otherwise, God would be a paternalistic God—the kind of God that, as we have already said, cannot be God. 'And if we are children [of God] we are heirs as well: heirs of God and coheirs with Christ, sharing his sufferings so as to share his glory' (Rom. 8:17). But Jesus goes even further. Just as we are responsible for the realisation of creation, so too are we responsible for the actualisation of the Redemption. It is up to us to bring salvation to mankind and to the universe.

And so, the Redemption, which has been lived by Jesus, the Head of the body of humanity, must now be realised, day by day, in the members of that body. But just as the mystery of the Creation and of the Incarnation of Jesus Christ can be complete only with man's free assent, the mystery of the Redemption can become effective only through the full and loving consent of each one of us: 'In my own body [I] do what I can to make up all that has still to be undergone by Christ for the sake of his body, the Church' (Col. 1:24). What is missing from the sufferings of Christ is not human suffering; he has already accepted, borne, and offered human suffering to the Father. What is missing is that we freely give him our suffering, and that, in him and with him, we offer our suffering for the salvation of the world.

We Christians, therefore, must not make a mere pious memory of Christ's passion. The 'way of the Cross' is not a spiritual exercise suitable for those tender souls who are more concerned with the past than with the present and the future. The true Way of the Cross is not finished, for it has two dimensions. In one dimension, it was completed by Jesus Christ two thousand years ago, in the streets of Jerusalem. In the second dimension, however, the Way of the Cross is being followed by the whole of humanity, by all the members of Jesus Christ. This Way of the Cross comprises all the streets of humanity, all the paths of history and of time. It runs through man's torn body, through his divided heart, through his convulsed being. It passes through divided couples, destroyed families. It passes through the world of labour, and through the organisation or disorganisation of labour by which man is made a slave. It passes through the lines of the unemployed, through understaffed and inadequate schools, through slums, hospitals, prisons. It passes through underdeveloped countries. It passes through the battlefields. It passes everywhere that there is suffering, great or small, since all suffering affects man and strikes at the total body of humanity.

The cross dominates the world and time as it dominated Jerusalem. For sin too remains and unfolds in time, just as the Redemption is a divine and continuing action—an uninterrupted mystery of love which shall last as long as the race of man....

The mystery of the Redemption is also the mystery of the Resurrection, for the Way of the Cross does not end at the tomb, but continues beyond death and leads to the joy of life eternal. Jesus Christ is the great conqueror of sin, suffering, and death. In him, every man, and all of mankind—past, present, and future—are dead and brought to life again: God 'brought us to life with Christ—it is through grace that you have been saved—and raised us up with him and gave us a place with him in heaven, in Christ Jesus' (Eph. 2:5-6). And so, there is no one, no sin, not a moment of our lives, not a particle of the universe, which is not affected by Christ's victory. Nothing is outside the Redemption which has been accomplished. He has gathered all things within himself: man, humanity, the world. He has offered all things, given all things, made all things 'happen' in God; and all things have been restored to life.

If we are willing, every moment of our lives can resound with the joy of Easter. And the true Christian cannot live without joy. He is given over to joy. In his life there can be no enduring failure—neither suffering nor death are insurmountable obstacles for him. Everything is the raw material of redemption, of resurrection, for, in the middle of his sufferings and his deaths, Christ the Conqueror waits. If a Christian is unhappy, it can only be because he has succumbed to the temptation to flirt with death and to turn his back on life. For that reason, the greatest suffering and the greatest joy can coexist in the same life and be intimately interconnected. By 'joy' we do not mean the transient (though legitimate) pleasure that comes from comfort, or the false happiness of the simple mind that is unaware of his degradation, or the 'virtuous' resignation of a psuedomystic, or the blind optimism of the man who figures that 'it is better to laugh than to cry.' We mean rather the calm, the interior serenity, and the profound peace which permeate and emanate from a man who, notwithstanding a torn heart and body, and despite the suffering of mankind and the world, believes with all his strength in the victory of the Saviour. And he believes this without for an instant forgetting or denying the existence of suffering and sin, and without giving up the fight against them.

The man who has entered into this joy and remains in it becomes, in Christ, what the Father wants him to be. He has reached his true level, as a man who is totally developed; for he has reached the ultimate stage in his communion with the Mystery of Jesus—not only the mystery of Creation; not only the mystery of Incarnation; not only the mystery of Redemption. But also the mystery of *Resurrection.— Christ is Alive!* (Dublin, Ireland: Gill and Macmillan Ltd. 1971), pp. 93-94, 105-106.

UNIT 10—Pressing on Toward the Goal/Philippians 3:12-4:1

Ready

In the last unit Paul identified his driving passion. It was to know Jesus Christ. In this unit he tells us about the process by which he seeks to achieve this goal of knowing Christ fully. Put simply: it is by *striving constantly* to understand and experience all that Christ is. In the course of describing the pattern by which he lives—in contrast to the life pattern of the Jewish teachers in Philippi—Paul says some very interesting things about what it means to live like a Christian. Surprisingly, what he says about the Christian life is not always what we expect him to say or even what we would like him to say. For example, he says:

☐ Try as hard as you like, you will never succeed in reaching the goal of knowing Jesus fully—at least not in this life.

☐ In order to move toward this goal of knowing Christ in his fullness, the Christian must "press on" and "strain forward." Knowing Christ ever more fully happens neither easily nor automatically.

☐ The basic pattern for the Christian life is found in the two-fold movement of *forgetting the past* (lest we be weighed down by guilt or pride) and *striding wholeheartedly into the future* (confident of all that has been promised us as children of God).

☐ Not all Christians will agree with this, he knows. Some feel that perfection in the present *is* possible, but according to Paul, God will reveal to them that they are wrong.

☐ Christian leaders ought to model this lifestyle.

☐ There are other ways of viewing the religious life. Paul identifies one such alternate pattern—that of the Jewish leaders in which ritual observance is paramount.

☐ Our ultimate hope is that our frail and unrealiable bodies will be transformed into something quite new and wonderful—akin to the "glorious body" of Christ.

In other words, what Paul is saying is that a Christian pattern of living does actually exist. Specifically, we are to be pilgrims striding confidently into the future in the process of which we grow in the depth of our comprehension of Jesus Christ on all levels of our personality. To be a Christian is to be on the move all the time, striving for the wholeness we see in Jesus Christ. The Christian is a pilgrim.

But here is the rub. A lot of us would rather be settlers. We prefer a nice comfortable faith which we can live out quietly within the confines of a safe Christian community. We'd rather not have to keep at this business of growing.

Pilgrim or settler? This is the choice and it is a real one. This is what you are going to discuss in your session today. Your aim as teacher is two-fold. You want to help folks see clearly the two options: what is a pilgrim and what is a settler. And then you want to create the kind of atmosphere in which it becomes possible for people to assess honestly the pattern that characterizes their own Christian walk.

Aim

☐ To understand the pattern Paul gives for Christian living . . . and so grasp what life is like with Christ at the center.

☐ To understand the two parts of this pattern . . . and then to discuss what it means on a personal level to forget the past and embrace the future.

☐ To reflect on what happens when we imagine that we have gained perfection in our Christian life . . . and so better understand Paul's rejection of this as a possibility.

☐ To examine what it means to be a pilgrim or a settler in our Christian lifestyle . . . and thus to understand better the dynamics of our own lives.

Fire

Begin this session by saying: "What is the Christian life all about? What is the basic pattern that is meant to characterize our daily walk? What lies behind the various guidelines in the Bible that give us direction as to how we ought to relate to the world around us?

"Have you ever wondered about questions like this? Today, in this passage, we are going to look at Paul's answer to these questions. We are going to examine what he says about the core pattern of the Christian life.

(A) "You remember how he came to be dealing with this whole question of the nature of Christian living. (B) All this comes in the context of his warnings about the false teachers who were bothering the folks at Philippi. In the last unit, you remember, after calling these Jewish missionaries a few uncomplimentary names, Paul then pinpoints the error in their teaching. They think that it is possible by scrupulous ritual observance to earn the right to go to heaven. Now, Paul knows this is wrong. If anyone would have made it into heaven by his own efforts, Paul would have been the guy. He lists his rather formidable religious credentials. But then he evaluates these in light of his experience in Jesus Christ. All that he was and all that he did was mere "rubbish" in light of knowing Jesus Christ. "Rubbish," as you know, is a polite translation of a rather crude word that Paul uses to describe his past. Paul's language here is spicy, to say the least. In any case, after saying all this, Paul then reflects on what it means to him to have come to know Christ. As we read his words in 3:7-11, we feel his deep passion, his heart-felt yearning to know Christ fully.

"All this brings us to our present unit. Having identified the central element in his life—knowing Christ, here in this passage he tells us what this means in practical terms. How does a person come to know Christ in an ever fuller way? Not that he will ever fully comprehend Christ. He is emphatic on this point. He knows that perfection is not possible. Far from it. There is so much to Jesus that he can never grasp it all in one lifetime. But what Paul can do is to *press on* and *strain forward,* ever seeking to know Christ better, forgetting about his past and keeping his eyes fully on the future.

"This, then, is the pattern for Christian living. It is a pressing forward to know Christ while simultaneously forgetting about past successes and failures that might weigh one down with either pride or guilt.

"This is the pattern and it is crucial for us to grasp it if we are able to understand this unit. It is crucial for us to grasp this pattern if we are to understand how to live as Christians. Let's begin then by reviewing what Paul says in 3:12 to 4:1 about the dynamic of the Christian life."

Discuss

The Pattern
Continue your lecture by first reading through the text and then by sharing one by one the points made in the **Ready** section. You might wish to list these points on the chalkboard as you lecture.

Ask: Why is it important to forget the past and look to the future in our Christian lives? Answers will include:

☐ Past failure can so overwhelm us that we never get on with the present, much less with the future.

☐ Past success can tempt us to think that we really can make it on our own. We might be deluded into thinking that we can lead the kind of lives that will make us fit candidates for heaven and thus feel that we do not need the grace of God.

☐ With our eyes looking back over our shoulders we are apt to stumble as we try to move forward.

☐ With our eyes on the future we live in hope of what can and will be, and thus our attitude is positive.

☐ To focus on past failures can make us pessimistic and unwilling to step out into new challenges, while to focus on the future brings optimism and energy.

Ask: From your own experience, can you give examples of what it means to live in the past in contrast to what it means to live with a future orientation? How has this impacted your spiritual life?

The Problem of Perfection
Begin by commenting: "In contrast to this pattern of constant growth toward a future goal Paul points out a different pattern of living. In this other scheme it was thought possible to experience spiritual perfection in the here and now. The path by which one gained such perfection varied from group to group. Some groups said that perfection came as a result of rigorous observance of a set of standards (the Jews). Others said it came when a person was given the "secret" of living by those who were already perfect (the mystery religions). Paul, of course, disagrees with both ideas and rejects out of hand the possibility of perfection. ("Not that I have already obtained all this, or have already been made perfect . . ." is how he puts it in verse 12.) However, even today, within certain Christian circles there are those who feel that it is possible to be perfect."

Ask: What is the effect on *us* when we feel that we must be perfect if we are Christians? Answers will include:

☐ We may become depressed by our inconsistencies and shortcomings even when we are trying hard.

☐ We are tempted to explain away and rationalize our failures with the result that we can never deal with them.

☐ We might become proud and arrogant over our successes.

☐ We might thus adopt a patronizing air and start acting superior to others.

Ask: What is the effect on *others* when we feel that we are perfect (or close to it)? Answers will include:

☐ Some people will avoid us because we make them feel inferior.

☐ Other people are amused by our pretension.

☐ Still others feel judged by us.

☐ Few feel encouraged to be like us.

Pilgrim or Settler?
Share the following: "There are two ways of looking at the Christian life. Either it is an ongoing pilgrimage in which we are constantly growing and always learning more about Christ. Or, it is more akin to a settled life in which we simply go on reaffirming the old truths but never venturing out on the basis of these truths into new areas of growth and ministry. Pilgrim or settler? A dynamic or a static lifestyle? This is the choice that confronts us as Christians. Listen to how

these two options are described in the book *Pilgrimage*.

Read aloud the article entitled "The Settler and the Pilgrim" found in the **Comment** section.

Ask: In assessing your own experience, would you say that you have tended to be more like a pilgrim or more like a settler? Why?

Remind
Homework

Comment

The Settler and the Pilgrim
by Richard Peace

Are we actually pilgrims or really just settlers? How can I tell whether my basic orientation to life is that of a pilgrim or that of a settler? What is a settler after all? What does this lifestyle look like? What attitudes characterize him?

The most important characteristic of a settler is that he has stopped moving; or at least he has limited his movements of growth to a fairly well-defined sphere. In other words, he has found a "position," claimed it as his own, and settled down to live within its confines.

I don't think most of us intend to become settlers. It is just that at some point we find ourselves in a really congenial atmosphere. We feel comfortable there. We fit. We are accepted. We share the group's beliefs, tastes, and ways of looking at the world. So, we stop. Sure, we may not be learning much that is new nor having any particularly meaningful spiritual experience... but by and large, we are content.

And it's easy to understand *why* we stop. There are many advantages to the life of a settler over that of a pilgrim. It's cold and dangerous out there in the world as a pilgrim. There is no telling who you might meet and how they might influence you. The world is a dangerous environment filled with wrong, even Satanic ideas, that do have power in and of themselves. Whereas in a secure environment, with well-defined and well-defended boundaries, there is a sort of peace.

Boundaries are very important for the settler. They are the things that give shape and definition to his existence. They also define for him the people with whom he can safely associate, the ideas he can espouse, and the activities he can enjoy....

The idea of pilgrimage is a central concept in the Old Testament. It was by means of a pilgrimage that the nation of Israel began. Abraham left his home in Ur and ventured out into the unknown because God called him to do so, the end result of which was the founding of a new nation. It was by means of another pilgrimage that this nation, now quite large, left its slavery and came into a land of its own. Even today the Exodus from Egypt is remembered and celebrated....

I believe there are at least three distinguishing marks that characterize a Christian pilgrim. The first, and perhaps most distinctive quality, is that of *movement*. A pilgrim is an individual who has embarked on a journey of growth. Second, a pilgrim is characterized by his awareness of a *goal*. He is not involved in aimless wandering but rather in progressing purposefully toward a very distinctive, very real objective. Finally, a pilgrim is characterized by his willingness to pay the price such a life-style requires. He keeps moving toward his goal, despite the difficulty and pain that this sometimes involves....

As the very image itself connotes, the pilgrim is a man in motion. He is an individual who is restless to learn. To my mind, it is this restlessness which sets a modern pilgrim apart from his fellows, who all too often live their whole lives based solely on what they learn in the early years of life. The pilgrim does not disparage the truths he learned while growing into adulthood, but rather yearns to find out what lies behind them, why they are true, how they apply in different areas of life. He wants to understand as much about them as he can. He wants to live them and experience them. Truth, for the pilgrim, is not a static statement. It is more like a many-faceted jewel which when held up to the light reveals ever new configurations and colors. The pilgrim longs to get to the essence of what is true in all its multi-faceted brilliance....

There is a second distinguishing characteristic of a pilgrim. He has a goal toward which he journeys....

It is this matter of a goal that marks the difference between a pilgrim and a spiritual vagabond. From time to time one meets those individuals who bustle from spiritual concern to spiritual concern. One month they are hyperactive in a *koininia* group. The next month they are enthusiastic charismatics. In a short time they drop this interest and get involved in organizing a boycott. Here is activity and movement, but it is undirected. The spiritual vagabond flits from activity to activity, searching, almost desperately, for meaning, for "spiritual thrills," or for an experience that will make him "better" than someone else. He is not in touch yet with what God wants to bring about in his life. Until that happens, his activity will never become a pilgrimage....

The pilgrim has a goal: to dwell in the presence of God as a whole person. It is a goal that draws him ever onward.... He cannot escape the restless longing to grasp it. He is indeed lured by things beyond. — *Pilgrimage: A Handbook on Christian Growth,* (Grand Rapids, MI: Baker Book House), 1984, pp. 7-8, 18-19, 22-24.

UNIT 11—Exhortations/Philippians 4:2-9

Ready

Two women are at war. And it has spilled over into the rest of the church. These are important women—leaders. Their opinions count. What they say has weight. Thus their conflict is devastating. But who is right? Who is to be followed? Some of the Christians choose one side. Longstanding friends chose the other side. A lot of folks are caught in the middle. The situation is explosive. This is no ordinary quarrel. It has the potential to blow up the whole church.

Now, of course, we do not have enough historical detail to know if this is exactly what took place in Philippi. But we do have enough experience of contemporary church conflicts to know that it was not at all unlikely for this to have been the scenario. Human nature operates like this. Strong people in leadership roles do have an enormous impact on a body like the church. Perhaps you have lived through such a "war" in a church. Perhaps you were one of the central figures in the conflict.

Or perhaps this sort of conflict took place for you in a less public arena—like in your own home. In this case the two players were Mom and Dad. The issue . . . well, it was a compound of a hundred issues. All you know is that you and your two sisters were caught smack in the middle—especially you. Over time it became clear that Joyce had really joined your dad's team. She was the oldest and had always been special to him. And if forced to vote, it's clear that Molly would have come down on the side of Mom. But you could never choose. You didn't want to choose. You only wanted peace and harmony. You wanted to be a family again, and do fun things, like play and talk and travel and laugh together. The whole time, your deepest fear was that the quarrel would be made permanent. You worried a lot about whether Mom and Dad would get a divorce. Would the family dissolve? And then where would you all be?

This conflict-in-the-home scenario is all too real—vividly real for most all of us. If we have not gone through it ourselves, we have seen others go through it. We know all about the dynamics of divorce. And, of course, whatever the details of the situation at Philippi, in general terms, this is the very dynamic that was in operation, because a church is like a family. And a church split is like a divorce. Put yourself emotionally in the midst of a divorce and then transpose those feelings back to Paul and the church in Philippi. Then you will understand the passion behind his plea in this letter for unity.

You will also marvel at the subtlety and great skill with which Paul seeks to head off such a split. Think about how he did this. He begins his letter with a great outpouring of affection. He loves these folks. They are old friends, faithful friends. They are family. Then he focuses on *his* situation, not theirs. He talks about his passion for preaching the gospel. No hardship or pride can be allowed to stand in the way of this all consuming task. Then Paul switches his focus to their situation. He knows that they too share this same passion. They do not want their witness to be muted. But . . . and so he finally comes to the first problem facing them. They have enemies, false teachers who would lure them away from the gospel. These teachers must be resisted. But . . . and now he comes to the second problem confronting them. They will be unable to resist these foes unless they are united.

At this point Paul launches into a long, eloquent exposition about the dynamics of unity: what it is, how it is achieved, the way Jesus modeled for us the attitude of humility from which unity springs, the necessary response of the Christian if unity is to be experienced, etc. Next, he illustrates what he is talking about by means of three case studies. His relationship with Timothy and Epaphroditus forms the positive case. This is how Christians ought to relate. Then he looks at how Christians ought to relate to those who oppose the gospel. In this second case study he has come back to the external enemies that are bothering the Philippians.

Notice: up to this point virtually everything that Paul says about the problem within the Philippian church is indirect. It is still on the theoretical level. But then, in his third and final case study, he pinpoints the specific issue faced by the church: the quarrel between Euodia and Syntyche. This is the problem and it must be resolved. It will take the active work of both women—aided by the whole church, yoked together in a loyal fellowship. (I think Hawthorne is right in identifying the Philippian church as the mysterious Syzygus.)

The Philippians are going through a tough time. They have problems within and enemies without. So Paul finishes off what he has to say in this letter by laying out before them a set of attitudes that will enable them to "stand fast" in the midst of their adversity. With these words of encouragement, the core of the letter is complete. He quickly thanks them for their gift, sends greetings, and then signs off with the usual benediction.

What does all this mean? Just this: what looked at first glance like a simple folksy newsletter sent to good friends, devoid of any overriding theological concern, turns out to be as pointed and as passionate as any other of Paul's letters. It may be more subtle than the others and seemingly indirect, but nevertheless, it has a distinct, urgent purpose. So, it is not, after all, a casual letter dashed off to old friends because one of their number happens to be returning home shortly and so can act as the messenger.

Well, this has been a long introduction. You

won't be asked to use all this material directly in your class session today (unless you have extra time). But it is important that you as teacher grasp the flow of Philippians. It will give you an overview that will serve you well as you teach the book.

Your focus today is on the extraordinary conclusion to this unit in which Paul identifies a set of attitudes that will bring joy in the midst of hardship. This is the conclusion to his teaching on the theme of "joy" which has so pervaded the book of Philippians. He shows us here how joy is possible. He describes the mind-set that opens one to joy. So, this is where your teaching emphasis needs to be. However, this is not the last time you will discuss joy. In the final unit you will review and summarize the teachings of Paul about joy that are scattered over the course of the whole book.

Aim

☐ To examine the quarrel between Euodia and Syntyche . . . and thus grasp the core problem in the Philippian church and how Paul deals with it.

☐ To examine those attitudes that enable Christians to rejoice in difficult situations . . . and so grasp the basis on which Paul can both himself rejoice and urge others to rejoice.

☐ To reflect on the mind-set that Paul urges on us . . . and so come to see more clearly, in contrast, what our culture would have us think about.

Fire

Begin by saying: "With this section, Paul draws his letter to a close. He does, of course, write a few more lines before he signs off, but what he says in 4:10-23 is more by way of housekeeping details than anything else. It is in this unit that he completes what he really wants to say to the Philippians. He pinpoints for them the real problem they must deal with in their church: the conflict between the two women that is at the root of their disunity (or, perhaps, the most obvious reflection of it). And he concludes his teaching on joy by describing how they can know joy even in the midst of hardship. This is an extraordinary passage in terms of what he says about joy, and so we want to spend the bulk of our time with it. As a result we will take only a few moments to look at the quarrel that was so harmful to the church, and then we will focus for the rest of our time on the attitudes that bring joy."

Discuss

The Split

Begin by giving the following mini-lecture: "Paul now comes to the real issue in the Philippian church: the split between two strong leaders. This is the issue that he has been inching toward right from the beginning of his letter. This is why he has discussed in such detail the dynamics of unity. This is why he has illustrated so thoroughly what it takes to keep people together. Now he is ready to point to the specific problem in the church that must be mended if they are to be united and thus able to resist the false teachers. The problem has to do with the conflict between these two women who are evidently powerful forces in the church.

"Notice how cleverly Paul has done this. Rather than confronting the issue straightaway with the full weight of his apostolic authority, he eases his way toward the issue. He knows that if he confronted this problem head-on he might just blow up the whole church. Instead, he first lays the groundwork for what he wants to say—this is his extended discussion of unity. Then, he says what needs to be said quickly (in only two verses), gently, in love but with great power. And once he has brought the issue out into the open, he then leaves it and goes on to material that is of practical importance to the whole church; namely, how to find joy when there is pain."

[If you have time, you might want to explore this issue further by means of the questions below. But be sure to reserve adequate time for examining the mind-set that Paul urges here. This is really what is at the heart of his epistle.]

Ask: Have you ever been involved in a church split? Describe the experience. How would Paul's approach and his ideas on unity have helped in that situation?

Ask: Have you ever seen a family split up because the members were at war with one another? Describe the situation. How would Paul's approach and his ideas on unity have helped in that situation?

The Attitudes

Begin this section with these remarks: "Paul does not simply end his letter by begging Euodia and Syntyche to be reunited. He takes one further step. He commends to the church a set of attitudes which if followed will enable them to survive the tough times they are going through. These are the attitudes that enable the Christian to experience joy even though the circumstances are difficult. It is important to identify these attitudes since they are at the core of Paul's teaching about joy."

Ask: What attitudes does Paul commend to the Philippian church in verses 4-9 so that they will be able to stand firm in the face of adversity? Answers will include:

Eph 6:11-18   2 Cor 7

A - He urges them to *rejoice*. This rejoicing is to be "in the Lord" and "in all situations."

B - He urges them to *be gentle* in their dealings with others. They are not to stand fast on their "rights" but instead must be gracious and magnanimous toward others.

C - He urges them to *stop worrying* about their problems. To worry is to evidence a lack of confidence in God's care and power.

D - Instead of worrying he urges them rather to *pray with thanksgiving*. They are to bring the issues that trouble them to God.

E - Finally, he urges them to *think about* those positive moral virtues taught by their culture (v. 8) while simultaneously *putting into practice* the commands of God (v. 9).

Ask: In what way does each of these attitudes make it possible to live successfully in the midst of trial and conflict? [You might want to go over each of the points shown above in italics and see what people have to say. Or you can use the points below as the basis for a mini-lecture.] Answers will include:

A - When it becomes possible for you to rejoice, this is a sign that you have faced up to the adversity and have not allowed it to dominate you.

B - When people and circumstances are pressing in on you, the temptation is to stand on one's "rights." But this often creates a further reaction to you on the part of others—even if it is unjustified. Whereas, a gentle willingness to make allowances for others creates the climate in which resolution is possible.

C - Anxiety has no positive value. Fear and worry merely sap one's energy.

C - In contrast, offering your anxiety to God, confident that he will hear and that he is in control, is a positive, active way to deal with problems.

D - Furthermore, if one can do this with genuine thanksgiving (and not just reluctantly) this will open you to a new inner peace that will enable you to face the trial head on.

D - The peace of God is real and the experience of it drives away the doubts and fears, thus freeing one from their icy grip.

E - To focus one's thoughts on that which is good, right, and moral will generate the sort of perspective that will bring you through the trial. In this way you will have a sense of what to do and how to act.

E - Furthermore, if to this framework of general morality one adds faithful obedience to the ways of God, then you are as well prepared as possible to cope with what comes your way.

Summarize Paul's teaching in the following way: "Notice the implications of what Paul says here. Our basic attitude ought to be one of rejoicing rather than worrying. We can rejoice not because we are blind to difficulties or because God will somehow magically take our problems away. We can rejoice because we know that it is possible to offer all our anxieties to God in prayer. The implication is that God will hear and answer our prayers. God is in control, in other words, not circumstances. No matter how bleak it might be (and remember that both Paul and the Philippians were in tough situations) God is in control and God cares about us. So, not only can we bring our fears and problems to God in prayer, we can do so with thanksgiving. What we will experience as we do this is the peace of God. This peace, which like love is at the heart of God's nature, will stand guard over our inner self. That this is so or that this can be is beyond our understanding. It simply is. *This peace is the experiential base which makes joy possible.*

"Paul has more to say. So far we have only looked at the inner side of all this: what we do within and what we experience within. But Paul also says: treat others with great gentleness and magnanimity. The reason for this is clear. In times of stress we tend to snap at others. We have no energy beyond our own problem. We aren't open or gracious to others because we are feeling so stressed. This does not have to be the case. The same "peace of God" that calms inner fears can smooth relationships.

"There is something else we must do. We must control our thought life and must live in accord with Christian principles. This is the essence of what he says in verses 8 and 9. Peace and joy are not meant to be some sort of inner panacea that automatically protects us forever and which requires no further action on our part. Our peace and joy will be constantly threatened by negative input from our culture. We will talk more about this in a moment. Such inner experience is also no excuse for not acting in a responsible and moral way as we live our daily life. As we order our thought-life and as we live in a Christian manner, Paul assures us that 'the God of peace will be' with us. How exciting.

"So how does one find joy in hardship? Commit the situation to God in prayer. Let trust in God replace anxiety about the situation. Open yourself to the peace of God. This peace will be the ground upon which rejoicing is possible. You will know that God is alive, God is in control, and that no matter what happens, he will be with you. Thus you can genuinely rejoice."

Ask: Can someone illustrate from his or her life how these attitudes made it possible to deal with a difficult situation?

The Mind-Set
Begin with these comments: "Let's look a little more closely at verse 8. There Paul identifies the kind of mind-set or mental attitude that underlies not only joy but the whole of the Christian life. 'Think about such things,' Paul says. This is a very important verse since what Paul urges here by way of our thought life is quite different from what our society as a whole would have us think about.

"Consider for a minute what contemporary American culture urges us to fill our minds with. Look, for example, at what is on television. We spend an extraordinary amount of time watching television. (4½ hours a day for the average adult.) All that time cannot help but impact what we think about. What do we see on television?

- We are urged constantly to be *materialists*. Via the constant bombardment of ads we are cajoled to buy a seemingly endless parade of products, services, and 'experiences.' (The average high school student upon graduation will have witnessed some 350,000 commercials.)

- We are exposed to an enormous amount of *violence*. (The average graduating high school senior has witnessed 18,000 murders on television.) Violence is presented to us as the way to resolve conflict. The 'good guy' on television is often the one who is best at violence.

- We are exposed to a huge dose of *sexuality*. This comes not only on the cable channels (which are as explicit as can be) but on network shows which exploit sexuality as a way of attracting viewers.

"The list could go on. It might be interesting for you to reflect on what your mind is being fed daily—especially in light of what Paul urges us to fill our minds with. Let's make sure now that we are clear about what it is that Paul urges us to reflect upon."

Ask: What does Paul urge us to think about and what does each word or phrase mean? Answers will include:

- Whatever is *true*. Our thoughts need to focus on truth as it exists in the whole of life, not on error.

- Whatever is *noble*. Our thoughts need to be drawn to those things which command respect and move us beyond the mundane.

- Whatever is *right*. Our thoughts need to reflect on justice issues, on what is due to God and others.

- Whatever is *pure*. Our thoughts need to be on that which is unblemished and good, not on that which is dark and evil.

- Whatever is *lovely*. Our thoughts need to be on those people and things that draw forth love from us.

- Whatever is *admirable*. Our thoughts need to be on that which all know to be good and worthy of emulation.

- In sum, we need to fill our minds with those things that are morally *excellent* and universally *praised*.

Conclude with these remarks: "Our mind-set is important. Our mental attitude is crucial. In fact, I suspect that it is a negative mind-set that inhibits our experience of joy.

"Notice that although it is in verse 8 that Paul speaks directly to the question of our mind-set, in fact this whole discussion of attitudes is a discussion of mind-set. Rejoicing, thanksgiving, lack of anxiety, peace—all these are inner, mental experiences. You see what Paul is urging. He is commending a positive mind-set. We can cope if our mind is in the right place. There is great power to a positive mental attitude. In fact, I think that without such, rejoicing is impossible. Yet, how many of us live a negative life? We think about those things we do not like. We fill our minds with the trash our culture throws our way. We are preoccupied with our enemies, not our friends. No wonder we find it hard to rejoice! May the peace of God be our portion as we seek to fill our minds with that which upbuilds and encourages. May we be known as men and women of joy and peace."

Read, if you have time, by way of conclusion the wry comments of C. S. Lewis on how our mental state affects us. The selection which we have called "Diabolical Advice About Our Mental State" is taken from *The Screwtape Letters,* a book which purports to contain "letters from a senior to a junior devil." Make sure that your class knows what you are reading; and that when a reference is made to "the Enemy," Screwtape means "God."

Remind
Homework

Comment

Diabolical Advice About Our Mental State

by C. S. Lewis

Your patient will, of course, have picked up the notion that he must submit with patience to the Enemy's will. What the Enemy means by this is primarily that he should accept with patience the tribulation which has actually been dealt out to him—the present anxiety and suspense. It is about *this* that he is to say "Thy will be done," and for the daily task of bearing *this* that the daily bread will be provided. It is your business to see that the patient never thinks of the present fear as his appointed cross, but only of the things he is afraid of. Let him regard them as his crosses: let him forget that, since they are incompatible, they cannot all happen to him, and let him try to practise fortitude and patience to them all in advance. For real resignation, at the same moment, to a dozen different and hypothetical fates, is almost impossible, and the Enemy does not greatly assist those who are trying to attain it: resignation to present and actual suffering, even where that suffering consists of fear, is far easier and is usually helped by this direct action.

An important spiritual law is here involved. I have explained that you can weaken his prayers by diverting his attention from the Enemy Himself to his own states of mind about the Enemy. On the other hand fear becomes easier to master when the patient's mind is diverted from the thing feared to the fear itself, considered as a present and undesirable state of his own mind; and when he regards the fear as his appointed cross he will inevitably think of it as a state of mind. One can therefore formulate the general rule; in all activities of mind which favour our cause, encourage the patient to be un-selfconscious and to concentrate on the object, but in all activities favourable to the Enemy bend his mind back on itself. Let an insult or a woman's body so fix his attention outward that he does not reflect "I am now entering into the state called Anger — or the state called Lust." Contrariwise let the reflection "My feelings are now growing more devout, or more charitable" so fix his attention inward that he no longer looks beyond himself to see our Enemy or his own neighbours. — *The Screwtape Letters* (London: Collins/Fontana Books, 1942), pp. 34-36.

UNIT 12—Thanks for Their Gifts/Philippians 4:10-20

Ready

There is a fine line here somewhere between too much dependence and too much independence—and Paul struggles to pinpoint it in this unit. On the one hand, he is well aware that to be a Christian is to be part of a community. He knew that God was in the process of birthing sons and daughters all over the known world and molding them into a single family. Paul rejoiced in this fact. In his letter to the Ephesians he sings the praises of this universal church in almost rhapsodic tones. Being with one another and *depending* upon one another is what it means to be a Christian.

But there is another side to the coin. It was his very *independence* that enabled him to do the work to which God had called him. Because he was not tied down to one particular church, he could travel freely establishing churches everywhere. Because he took money from nobody, he could never be charged with promoting Christ "because of the money." The gospel came to him freely. He passes it along freely to others.

But Christians are supposed to be interdependent. Apostles ought to be supported by the churches. In this way they are freed up to be about the business of God—without undue worry about little things like food and shelter. In fact, Paul gives a vigorous defense of this "right" on the part of apostles (see 1 Corinthians 9:1-12a). However, after saying all this he then turns around and says that while all this is true in general, *he* will not, in fact, avail himself of this "right." It would get in the way of his preaching (1 Corinthians 9:12b-23). Paul was a very complex man!

So what about us? What about those of us who are ministers? Is it right to allow a congregation to support us? Or should we be bi-vocational: working part-time at a secular job so as to support our own ministry? This is the model in many black churches. Or as missionaries, should we expect the "folks back home" to keep on sending in the money to support our mission? Or should we become "tentmakers," like Paul. "Tentmaking" is a hot term in mission circles today. It is a relatively new way of doing missionary work whereby men and women go overseas to take up jobs offered by foreign firms and governments—using their specialized skills to assist the development of third-world countries, while simultaneously acting as missionaries—except that they receive no additional salary for this work. Tentmakers or faith missionaries? Which pattern is right?

The answer, of course, is that both patterns are right. Both are biblical. Both make sense. One fits better in certain circumstances. The other fits in different circumstances. One fits one person. The other fits a different sort of person. In other words, we too have a struggle with this issue the way St. Paul struggled with it. The significant thing about this unit is that we catch a glimpse of both sides of the issue. We hear Paul's ambiguity—and perhaps thereby better understand our own ambiguities.

Independence and dependence is one theme we will touch upon today, albeit in a rather cursory way. A second issue is the related question of wealth and poverty. We will spend more time on this one since it is of such wide application in our American environment. How much we give to missionaries like Paul relates to how much we have. How much we have relates to where on this planet we live. Since America is the richest nation on earth, we who are Americans must wrestle constantly with the issue of money and possessions.

The real issue is, of course, contentment—not wealth or poverty. It is far too easy for us as Americans to equate wealth with contentment. And yet we all know (or know about) miserable millionaires. And we know happy people who live below the poverty line. What is the root and source of contentment? What has Paul discovered that enables him to live as he does—in abundance or in poverty?

Aim

☐ To wrestle with the question of wealth and poverty in a world that is hungry . . . and so better understand Paul's perspective on materialism and on the nature of contentment.

☐ To try to understand the source of Paul's contentment . . . and learn how to live out of that same center.

☐ To note the tension between independence and dependence . . . and so face this issue in our own lives.

Fire

Begin by saying: "In today's passage Paul touches upon a raw nerve in American society: the issue of possessions. In describing why it is not necessary for the Philippians to send any more gifts to him, he articulates for us an attitude toward possessions that can guide us as we wrestle with the question of possessions and consumption as Christians in a world that is hungry. So today, we will first look squarely at this problem. What is the situation in the world at this point in time when it comes to consumption and possessions? Then second, we will make sure we have understood Paul's perspective. Finally, we will try to relate, on a personal and community level, Paul's perspective and the world's problem.

"First, then, what is the state of the world today in terms of food, fuel, and resources?

The statistics in this lecture are drawn from Ronald Sider's provocative book: *Rich Christians in an Age of Hunger—A Biblical Study* (InterVarsity Press) 1977."

Discuss

The Situation
Present the following mini-lecture: "Consider the following statements by Ron Sider:

☐ "Thirty percent of the world's population lives in the developed countries. But this minority of less than one-third eats three-quarters of the world's protein each year . . . 'At least 460 million are actually starving,' the U.N.'s *Development Forum* reported. That does not mean that they will die tomorrow of course. But it does mean that they get less than the minimum daily amount of needed calories. When this happens, one becomes listless and the body begins to burn up its own fats, muscles and proteins for energy. Tragically, even this ghastly figure of 462 million starving persons tells only part of the story. Experts think that another one-half to one and one-half billion persons lack adequate protein even though they eat enough calories" (pages 18, 32-33).

☐ "How long can the earth sustain the present rate of industrialization? What will be the effect of the resulting pollution? When will we run out of natural resources (especially fossil fuels such as coal and oil)? . . . A growing number of people agree with economist Robert Heilbroner: 'Ultimately, there is an absolute limit to the ability of the earth to support or tolerate the process of industrial activity, and there is reason to believe that we are now moving toward that limit very rapidly . . . In the developed world, industrial production has been growing at a rate of about 7 percent a year, thereby doubling every ten years. If we project this growth rate for another fifty years, it would follow that the demand for resources would have doubled five times, requiring a volume of resource extraction thirty-five times larger than today's; and if we look ahead over the ten doublings of a century, the amount of annual resource requirements would have increased by over a thousand times' " (pages 19-20).

☐ "In the developing countries one child in four dies before the age of five. The infant mortality rate there is ten times higher than in developed countries. And half of these deaths are related to inadequate diets" (p. 24).

"Many more statistics can be quoted. But they will only serve to confirm what is already abundantly clear: when it comes to consumption and possessions, there is an enormous imbalance between East and West, between North and South, between developing countries and developed countries. And it is also clear: as American Christians, we live on the consuming side of the equation. We have riches undreamed of in other countries. So, what ought our perspective to be? Do we sell all our goods and become poor ourselves? Do we simply ignore the unbalance? Is there a middle ground? Let's see if Paul has help for us."

Living in Poverty and Plenty
Ask: What does Paul say about the conditions of poverty and plenty? Answers will include:

☐ He has learned to be content in either circumstance.

☐ He has experienced both conditions: abject poverty when he did not have enough to eat and abundant wealth when he had far more than enough to eat.

☐ He has discovered the secret to existing in any circumstance: it is Jesus who gives him the strength to endure both conditions.

☐ Giving to others is a good thing to do (as the Philippians gave to him).

Ask: What are some of the implications of this perspective for us? [You may want to give this as a mini-lecture.] Answers will include:

☐ Paul does not pass judgment here on either condition. He does not say that to be wealthy or to be poor is the better position. (The question of wealth and poverty will have to be dealt with on the basis of other parts of Scripture.)

☐ He has lived as a Christian in both extreme wealth and utter poverty.

☐ Being content has nothing to do with having a lot or having a little. Contentment springs from another source.

☐ Paul does not seem to work actively either to stave off poverty or to accumulate wealth. His life motivation lies elsewhere. (It is to know Christ in his fullness—3:7-14, and to preach the gospel in all circumstances—1:12-30.)

☐ Both poverty and wealth are a potential threat to us, and we need the strength of Christ to enable us to cope in either circumstance.

Ask: What perspectives have been helpful to you in grappling with the question of how we as Christians ought to deal with the issue of wealth and poverty? How do these insights apply to how we live as individuals and as a church? [There are no "right" answers to these questions. Rather, seek to create a conversation in which honest searching and questioning can take place around the issues of consumption, possession, sharing, and stewardship.]

Contentment
Continue by saying: "When it comes right down to it, the issue is *contentment*. Paul says: 'I have learned the secret of being content in any and every situation . . .' Not a lot of us could say that, I suspect. There is nothing very mysterious about how Paul can say this. He reveals his 'secret' in verse 13: 'I can do everything through him who gives me strength.' Jesus is his secret—the indwelling, empowering, loving Lord of Lords makes it possible for Paul to thrive in whatever circumstance he finds himself.

"What it really boils down to is that Paul has found in Jesus a new center for his life. His life is no longer wrapped up in what happens around him. Circumstances are secondary. Jesus is primary. Jesus is the center of his life. Jesus is the source of his contentment. I suspect that until we make Jesus the center of our lives in this way we won't know this kind of contentment.

"This is not easy for us to do. Our whole culture cries out that happiness is found in having. Contentment comes on the heels of success. Our experience tells us that it is better to be well off financially than to have to struggle by on little. And yet . . . is this not making materialism the center of our life? Does that not make materialism a competing 'god' with the Lord God who wants our prime allegiance? And will we not continue to struggle with our own private discontent until we get this straight? It is so simple. Make Jesus Lord. Let your life revolve around knowing Jesus. And yet it is so hard for us. 'Let go and let Jesus,' the old cliché states. That is not at all easy. It is not the 'letting Jesus' that is the problem. It is the 'letting go' that is so hard. There is so much to let go of.

"In any case, I suspect it is not quite the either/or case the cliché would make it. Most of us are somewhere in between the two poles. We have not rejected Jesus in favor of materialism. But then neither are we holding fully to Jesus with no other center to our lives. We are struggling to keep on letting go and keep on letting Jesus. And this is the very path to contentment.

"Did you notice the connection between contentment and joy? The two are a lot alike. They are inner attitudes that are quite similar. They are both derived from knowing Jesus. They are both highly desirable. The difference lies in the affect connected to them. Joy is, well, a more 'joyous' experience, while contentment is a bit harsh and solitary, at least in the way the Stoics used it."

Ask: What is Paul's view of contentment? Compare and contrast this with the American view.

Dependence/Independence
If time remains, discuss the tension between being too dependent and being too independent, based on the comments in the **Ready** section.

Ask: At what points in your life do you wrestle with this tension? How have you resolved it or how are you dealing with it?

Remind

Homework
The whole question of the Christian's attitude to wealth and poverty is a complex one that is dealt with at various points in Scripture. Part II of Ron Sider's book considers a variety of these texts and is well worth studying in order to wrestle through to a Christian perspective on consumption.

UNIT 13—Final Greetings/Philippians 4:21-23

Ready

The letter to the Philippians is finished. Thus it is time to review the book by way of summary. In particular, it is important to look at the theme of joy. At the beginning of this course it was asserted that Philippians was a book about joy. At that time it was also clear that the "joy" about which Paul wrote was really quite different from "joy" as conceived by our culture. To us as twentieth-century Americans, "joy" is all too often equivalent to "satisfaction." To us, joy is the absence of hardship; joy is a feeling; joy is like the "happiness" that the United States Constitution tells us it is our "right to pursue." Clearly Paul had something quite different in mind when he wrote about joy in this letter. What, then, does Paul understand "joy" to be? What has he taught us about "joy" in the course of his letter to the Philippians? This is the prime question you will discuss today in this final session.

You have a secondary task as well. This is also the time when you will want to summarize the nature of your experience together as a class. Was this a good experience for all of you? Why or why not? What worked and what was not quite so successful? What was the nature of the learning? What made the most impact? What sort of changes took place in the thinking of people? In their attitudes? In their actions? What is the next step for all of you? You'll have a chance to explore some of these questions at the conclusion of the session.

There is another assessment which you ought to make: how well did you do as a teacher? Was this a good experience for you? A hard one? Easy? Boring? Creative? Fun? A pain? Try to assess how you feel about the past 13 (or 7) weeks. You will also want to assess what you learned about yourself as a teacher.

Are you a good teacher? A hesitant one? Do you dominate a class? Or are you so laid back that there is no control in the class? Do you find teaching easy or hard? Do you have command of the techniques of teaching? Are you comfortable and able in leading a large group discussion? Giving a lecture? Organizing a course? What about your own preparation? Did this come easily? Was this generally a last-minute proposition? Did you feel on top of the material? Work through these questions on your own. They are part of the process whereby you become an ever better teacher.

One last issue concerns what is on tap next for the class and for you as the teacher. Will you continue doing Bible study together? If so, what book will you study? After having studied Philippians—the most informal of Paul's epistles—it may be time to study Romans, which is the most tightly reasoned of his letters. Or you may want to follow up on this idea of the unity of the church which is so dominant in Philippians. In Ephesians Paul lays out in an almost vision-like way what he has discovered about God's cosmic plan for the unity of all creation beginning with the church. Or perhaps you need to look squarely at issues of lifestyle and behavior as discussed at length in 1 Corinthians, or in briefer form in James. In any case, do not lose the momentum of Bible study. The Bible really is God's Word and in it we not only learn how to live but we catch glimpses of the nature and work of God in the world.

Aim

☐ To explore the theme of "joy" as Paul expresses it in Philippians . . . and so grasp his definition of joy over against our cultural view of joy.

☐ To assess the impact of Philippians on each individual in the class . . . and so maximize the learning experience.

Fire

Begin by saying: "We have now come to the end of the Epistle to the Philippians. It has been an exciting journey through these chapters, filled as they are with the kind of insight that we need so that we can grow into the kind of people we long to be. We'll have a chance at the end of the session to share together some of what we have learned in these past weeks.

"First, however, we want to go back over Philippians and look at the central theme that pervades the whole book—the idea of joy. We touched on this theme when we began the course. But at that time we could do little more than get out into the open how our culture views joy. It was evident that our cultural definition of joy was not what Paul had in mind. For us, joy is more akin to an emotion we feel when things are going well than it is to anything else. It is what we experience in the flush of success or at times of high sensory excitement. Joy is to us often equivalent to happiness. But for Paul, joy had much more substance. It was, to be sure, a feeling, but it was more than a feeling. And it was present not just in good times but also in the midst of difficult times. In other words, while our culture knows in general what joy is, it is not fully in touch with how Paul understood this word.

"But now we have been through the whole book of Philippians. We've seen the church and come to understand the pressures it faced. We have seen Paul and the difficulties he faced. Most especially, we've heard Paul talk about joy in a variety of contexts. So we can go back over all this material in order to derive a definition of joy. Then we can reflect on what we have found and think about how joy can be our experience."

The Text
Continue: "Let's begin by noting once more the 19 times that Paul uses words that mean 'joy.' In fact, as you know, not all of these words which in Greek mean 'joy' (in one form or another) show up in our English translation. How these words are translated will become clear to you in a moment. The most common words Paul uses are the noun *chara* (5 times) and the related verb *chairein* (9 times) which refer to 'inward joy.' He uses the related word *sunchairein* twice which means 'shared joy.' And he uses the word normally translated 'boasting' three times (*kauchema* twice and *kauchasthai* once). These words carry the idea of 'justified boasting' or the 'joy of legitimate pride.' Here are the 19 times Paul speaks of 'joy' in Philippians." [If possible, make an overhead transparency of the verses below so that in the subsequent discussion you can easily refer to them.]

1:4 . . . I always pray with *joy*.
1:18 . . . The important thing is that in every way, whether from false motives or true, Christ is preached. And because of this I *rejoice*. Yes, and I will continue to *rejoice*.
1:25 . . . I know that I will remain, and I will continue with all of you for your progress and *joy* in the faith.
1:26 . . . your *joy (kauchema)* in Christ Jesus will overflow . . .
2:2 . . . make my *joy* complete by being like-minded . . .
2:15 . . . in order that I may *boast (kauchema)* on the day of Christ.
2:17 . . . But even if I am being poured out like a drink offering on the sacrifice and service coming from your faith, *I am glad*

(chairein) and *rejoice with (sunchairein)* all of you.
2:18 . . . So you too should *be glad (chairein)* and *rejoice with (sunchairein)* me.
2:28 . . . Therefore I am all the more eager to send him, so that when you see him again you may *be glad* and I may have less anxiety.
2:29 . . . Welcome him in the Lord with great *joy*.
3:1 . . . *rejoice* in the Lord!
3:3 . . . we who worship by the Spirit of God, who *glory (kauchasthai)* in Christ Jesus . . .
4:1 . . . my brothers, you whom I love and long for, my *joy* and crown . . .
4:4 . . . *Rejoice* in the Lord always. I will say it again: *Rejoice!*
4:10 . . . I *rejoice* greatly in the Lord that at last you have renewed your concern for me.

Discuss

The Analysis
Ask: In what ways does Paul indicate that joy is *not dependent* on circumstances? Answers will include:

☐ He writes this epistle of joy even though he himself is in prison.

☐ Several times he urges the Philippians to rejoice even though they are facing disunity from within and dissent from without.

☐ In 1:17-18 Paul says that it does not matter that certain Christians are preaching Christ out of selfish ambition, trying to stir up trouble for him while he is in jail. The important thing is that Christ is being preached. How people are treating him cannot diminish his joy.

☐ In 2:17, Paul says that even though he might be sacrificed, his joy will not be diminished.

Ask: In what ways does Paul indicate that joy *can be affected* by circumstances? Answers will include:

☐ In 2:2 Paul says that the Philippians can make his joy complete by heeding his call to unity.

☐ In 2:27-29 Paul says that he would have experienced waves of sorrow (the opposite of joy) had Epaphroditus actually died. But, since he lives, his return to Philippi will bring them great joy.

Ask: In what ways is joy an emotion? In what ways is joy a form of knowledge? In what ways is joy a behavior? Answers will include:

Emotion.

☐ 2:28-29—The return of Epaphroditus will bring feelings of joy to his friends.

☐ 4:10—When the Philippians got back in touch with Paul this brought feelings of joy to Paul.

Viewpoint.

☐ In 4:4-7 Paul identifies the reasons why they can rejoice. Here he reminds them that the Lord is near. Jesus will come again soon, but even at that moment he is present in their lives. (They are "in Christ Jesus.") Thus they can bring all anxiety to the Lord in prayer. In response, God will bring peace to their hearts and minds. For those who have this viewpoint it becomes possible to rejoice in times of pain as well as in times of pleasure.

Behavior

☐ Rejoicing is a form of behavior that shows itself both in words and actions. Paul writes about his joy. We verbalize joy. Joy even shows itself in our bodies.

- Paul urges them to rejoice (2:18; 3:1; 4:4).
- Paul himself rejoices (1:18; 2:17; 4:10). Rejoicing is something you do. It is an action.

Ask: How would you define the way in which Paul understands the word "joy"? [Use this time to draw together the various strands of the discussion into a coherent understanding of what joy is in Paul's view.]

The Response
Ask: What does Paul's call to rejoice mean to us? What does this mean in terms of how you feel, how you think, and how you behave?

Read: If you have time, you might want to read the essay in the **Comment** section which describes C. S. Lewis' "Search for Joy." This is a theme which is related (though not identical) to Paul's discussion of joy.

The Assessment
Use the remainder of the time to evaluate the course experience. In terms of the ideas in the course:

Ask: What other themes did you note in the Epistle to the Philippians? Which theme was the most important to you? What was the key concept for you? The key verse? If you were asked to describe in a sentence or two what Philippians is all about, what would you say?

Ask: What did you learn from this study that changed how you think, feel, or behave?

Ask: What book should we study next?

End the class with prayer together in which you commit this whole experience to God.

Comment

The Search for Joy
C. S. Lewis, the famous Oxford scholar and writer, was a man whose whole life was lived in search of joy. His autobiography is entitled *Surprised by Joy,* and, curiously enough, when he married late in life, it was to a woman by the name of Joy. This "joy" that Lewis both sought and found is not exactly the "joy" about which Paul wrote, though the two are connected. For Lewis, the joy he sought was more akin to "longing" than anything else—"an inconsolable longing" as he calls it in one of his sermons. When he wrote about this "joy" he would often capitalize it. Such "Joy" made itself known in those rare but powerful moments when there welled up within one an almost overwhelming sense that there is more to reality than we yet know, that we were meant to be part of that larger reality, and that to touch that reality is to touch God. These flashes of intuition are triggered in a variety of ways—by music, by a phrase in a book or a line of poetry, by a sunset over a Canadian lake, by a child. Listen to how Lewis speaks of this:

> In speaking of this desire for our own far-off country, which we find in ourselves even now, I feel a certain shyness. I am almost committing an indecency. I am trying to rip open the inconsolable secret in each one of you—the secret which hurts so much that you take your revenge on it by calling it names like Nostalgia and Romanticism and Adolescence.
> Our commonest expedient is to call it beauty and behave as if that had settled the matter. Wordsworth's expedient was to identify it with certain moments in his own past. But all this is a cheat. If Wordsworth had gone back to those moments in the past, he would not have found the thing itself, but only the reminder of it; what he remembered would turn out to be itself a remembering. The books or the music in which we thought the beauty was located will betray us if we trust to them; it was not in them, it only came *through* them, and what came through them was longing. These things—the beauty, the memory of our own past—are good images of what we really desire; but if they are mistaken for the thing itself they turn into dumb idols, breaking the hearts of their worshippers. For they are not the thing itself; they are only the scent of a flower we have not found, the echo of a tune we have not heard, news from a country we have never yet visited.[1]

Lewis talks about this "Joy" in his autobiography:

> I had tried everything in my own mind and body; as it were, asking myself, "Is it this you want? Is it this?" Last of all I had asked if Joy itself was what I wanted; and, labelling it "aesthetic experience," had pretended I could answer Yes. But that answer too had broken down. Inexorably Joy proclaimed, "You want—I myself am your want of—something other, outside, not you nor any state of you." I did not yet ask, Who is the desired? only What is it? But this brought me already into the region of awe, for I thus understood that in deepest solitude there is a road right out of the self, a commerce with something which, by refusing to identify itself with any object of the senses, or anything whereof we have biological or social need, or anything imagined, or any state of our own minds, proclaims itself sheerly objective. Far more objective than bodies, for it is not, like them, clothed in our senses; the naked Other, imageless (though our imagination salutes it with a hundred images), unknown, undefined, desired.[2]

---

[1] C. S. Lewis, *Transposition and Other Addresses* (London: Geoffrey Bles, 1949), pp. 23-24.
[2] *Surprised by Joy: The Shape of My Early Life* (NY: Harcourt, Brace & World, Inc., © 1955 by C. S. Lewis) pp. 220-221.

Is this longing for Joy the same as the joy Paul experiences and describes in Philippians? It is not dissimilar. Lewis' Joy is close to the longing which Paul articulates in chapter one—this great desire to leave the body and so be with the Lord.

"What shall I choose? I do not know! I am torn between the two: I desire to depart and be with Christ, which is better by far; but it is more necessary for you that I remain in the body. Convinced of this, I know that I will remain, and I will continue with all of you for your progress and joy in the faith...."[3]

Compare this to Lewis: "There have been times when I think we do not desire heaven; but more often I find myself wondering whether in our heart of hearts, we have ever desired anything else."[4]

It is, indeed, the desire for heaven—where Joy is ultimately found—that Lewis calls our inconsolable longing. And certainly, at the root of Paul's joy is his sure knowledge that he is in Christ and Christ is in him. "The Lord is near," Paul declares in Philippians 4:5. And because this is so—because of this New Reality—life in the here and now is given perspective. Thus we can rejoice even when life is difficult. The flashes of Joy that Lewis experiences and which create within him the hope of one day being a part of that Joy are not dissimilar to the joy Paul knows and lives in. Our joy now is derived from the Joy that is beyond. Our knowledge and experience of joy is bound tightly to Jesus who is, ultimately, Joy itself.

[3] Philippians 1:22-25
[4] *The Problem of Pain*, (London: Collins, Fontana Books, 1957 edition) p. 133.

ACKNOWLEDGEMENTS

In preparing these notes, generous use was made of the traditional tools of New Testament research: *A Greek-English Lexicon of the New Testament* by Arndt & Gingrich; *Dictionary of New Testament Theology*, edited by Colin Brown, *The NIV Complete Concordance*, various New Testament "Introductions," etc. In addition, use was made of a variety of commentaries. While it is not possible, given the scope and aim of this book, to acknowledge in detail the influence of each author, the sources of direct quotes and special insights are noted. The key commentary used in the preparation of these notes is *Philippians* by Gerald F. Hawthorne, (Word Biblical Commentary, Volume 43), Waco, TX: Word Books, 1983. This commentary had not been published when the first draft of these notes was written in 1981. However, it aided greatly in the expansion and revision of the materials in 1985. Other commentaries frequently consulted include: *Philippians* by Ralph P. Martin (The New Century Bible Commentary), Grand Rapids, MI: Wm. B. Eerdmans Publishing Co., 1976; *Philippians* by F. F. Bruce (A Good News Commentary), San Francisco: Harper & Row, 1983; *A Translators Handbook on Paul's Letter to the Philippians* by I-Jin Loh and Eugene A. Nida (Helps for Translators), United Bible Societies, 1977; *The Letters to the Philippians, Colossians, and Thessalonians* by William Barclay (The Daily Study Bible), Edinburgh: The Saint Andrew Press, 1959; and *Joy in the New Testament* by William Morrice, Grand Rapids, MI: Wm. B. Eerdmans, 1984.

Reference was also made to *Paul's Letters from Prison: Philippians, Colossians, Philemon, and Ephesians* by J. L. Houlden (Westminster Pelican Commentaries), Philadelphia: The Westminster Press, 1970, 1977; *A Critical and Exegetical Commentary on the Epistles to the Philippians and to Philemon* by Marvin R. Vincent (The International Critical Commentary) Edinburgh: T. & T. Clark, 1897; *The Message of Philippians: Jesus our Joy*, by Alec Motyer (The Bible Speaks Today), Downers Grove, Ill.: InterVarsity Press, 1984; *Philippians: Jesus our Joy* by Donald Baker (A Lifebuilder Bible Study) Downers Grove, Ill.: InterVarsity Press, 1985; *The Epistles of Paul to the Philippians and to Philemon* by Jac J. Müller (The New International Commentary on the New Testament) Grand Rapids, MI: Wm. B. Eerdmans Publishing Co., 1955, 1980; and *Philippians and Colossians: Letters from Prison* by Marilyn Kunz and Catherine Schell (Neighborhood Bible Studies), Wheaton, Ill.: Tyndale House Publishers, 1972.

Special thanks go to John Crosby whose research was of great assistance in the preparation of the first draft of this material. Thanks are also due to Carrie Powell who typed the first draft and to Tina Howard who assisted with the final draft. Thanks also go to Dr. Gordon Fee, Professor of New Testament at Gordon-Conwell Theological Seminary, who serves as technical consultant to the project.

Copyright Endorsements

Grateful acknowledgement is made to the following publishers for permission to reprint copyright material:

Units 5 and 7
INTERVARSITY PRESS for excerpts from *The Flight* by John White. Copyright © 1976 by InterVarsity Christian Fellowship of the USA and used by permission of InterVarsity Press, P.O. Box 1400, Downers Grove, IL 60515.

Unit 6
COLLINS PUBLISHERS for excerpts from *Miracles* by C. S. Lewis. Copyright © 1960 by William Collins Sons and Company, Ltd., Glasgow G64 2QT, Great Britain. Used by permission.